Twenty-five years of *Stagecoach*

Doug Jack

Ian Allan PUBLISHING

Contents

Front cover: Two of the most high-profile Stagecoach operations are the Oxford Tube and Megabus.com express coach services. In 2004/5 these were upgraded by the introduction of 50 13.7m Neoplan Skyliners. Megabus 50131 (SV54 ELW) passes Oxford Tube 50113 (KP04 GKD) in Central London.

Back cover (upper): Since 1996 Stagecoach has held the South West Trains rail franchise, providing services throughout West Surrey, Hampshire and Dorset. Class 442 'Wessex Electric' unit No 2420 is seen approaching Southampton on 27 May 2004 with a Weymouth-Waterloo service. *Brian Morrison*

Back cover (lower): Through its Coach USA subsidiary Stagecoach runs the Gray Line sightseeing operation in New York, for which 20 Dennis Tridents were bought new in 2002.

Title page: A brand-new Dennis Trident from the East Midland fleet is seen in the unlikely location of London's Trafalgar Square. This was one of a number of buses loaned to Selkent to cover for the temporary removal from service of that company's Mercedes-Benz Citaro articulated buses, after a number of the latter type (none owned by Stagecoach) had suffered catastrophic engine fires.

Right: Stagecoach double-deckers can be found on some relatively long rural routes. Delivered in 1991, Cumberland 1025 (J125 XHH) was a standard long-wheelbase Leyland Olympian with Alexander bodywork. It had 74 coach seats instead of the 87 bus seats often fitted to this model and is seen amid typical Lakeland scenery in February 2001.

First published 2005

ISBN 0 7110 3103 7

Published by Ian Allan Publishing

an imprint of Ian Allan Publishing Ltd, Hersham, Surrey KT12 4RG.

Printed in England by Ian Allan Printing Ltd, Hersham, Surrey KT12 4RG.

Code: 0506/B

Foreword

IF a week is a long time in politics, then it is probably fair to say that 25 years is a lifetime in business. Indeed, the past quarter century has seen massive developments in the public transport industry and a transformation in the scale of Stagecoach.

Stagecoach has come a long way since 1980 when my sister, Ann, and I started the company with just two buses in the city of Perth in Scotland. From the early days of running coach services from Scotland to London, through the purchase of former National Bus Company businesses, the expansion overseas, our move into rail and other transport modes, to our revitalised position today, it has been an exciting and eventful journey.

Our company has moved from being the youthful upstart of the transport industry, born out of deregulation, to become an established and mature business. However, Stagecoach has lost none of its drive and passion for new ideas in the transport business.

We have always had a very clear strategy and we have been pioneers in the industry — seeking out new markets, setting high standards and always striving to be the best. That has been as true from our early development of the Magicbus concept as it is today in our use of the web and e-commerce on products such as our low-cost inter-city service, megabus.com.

The common thread running through the story of Stagecoach is innovation: market-leading thinking, cutting-edge research and development and a flair for marketing. From new products to the use of new technology, we have been pioneers. Some of the first Stagecoach marketing drew on the Wild West theme for its inspiration, and in one way our experience has been like these early settlers seeking out new territories.

Of course, not all of our adventures have been without their challenges, but there is a lot of truth in the old saying, 'nothing ventured, nothing gained'. Without taking calculated risks and exploring new ventures, we would never have grown to become the company we are today.

While Stagecoach has grown dramatically over the past 25 years, we have remained true to our culture and our conviction that a lean management structure and short chains of command are the best way of delivering effective and efficient services. That approach has brought us success on both buses and railways.

Starting something new in business is always a challenge, and one factor above all else has been most important to Stagecoach over the past quarter century: people. New ventures don't just happen by themselves. They take planning, attention to detail and bag-loads of enthusiasm. At Stagecoach, we can run with ideas quickly because we have motivated and productive people.

Without the great people of Stagecoach — many of whom have been with the company since the early years — we would not be where we are today. Our success is a tribute to their talent and commitment. That is why here, as we celebrate the past, I have confidence that the future of Stagecoach is in good hands.

Brian Souter

Introduction

THE fact that Stagecoach has reached the age of 25 years is a fitting response to those who predicted in the early days that the newcomer would not survive 25 weeks — or, if slightly less uncharitable, 25 months! It is a remarkable story of a company that started in Perth and, in its infancy, quickly took advantage of the opening-up of previously closed markets, offered by deregulation, to develop a network of express coach services.

Stagecoach has always been a pioneer. For the first 15 years or so it was run by Brian Souter and Ann Gloag, brother and sister, who to this day retain major shareholdings. Ann retired from her executive role about six years ago but remains a valued non-executive director. Brian is the strategist, always thinking about ways to develop the business. He has the rare ability to see the big picture and predict future trends with remarkable accuracy, but he can also home in on the revenue from just one route. He is also rare, among chief executives, in being able to turn his hand to practically any job in the company, except a mechanic or train driver. Indeed, he has an almost humble approach, especially when meeting someone for the first time, but he has charm and humour and knows exactly what he wants out of any conversation. Ann is more assertive, but again with a wonderful sense of humour. There have been people who have underestimated Brian and Ann over the years, and their ears should have burned afterwards. Both are great mimics and can easily slip into other accents when recounting meetings!

Brian and Ann worked as a team to build up Stagecoach. They divided their responsibilities but, as Ewan Brown, their first (and still serving) non-executive director, said, they had an instinctive management relationship. Each knew what the other was doing and each could do the other's job if necessary. They have the ability to talk to absolutely anyone, being equally at ease talking to drivers and passengers or high-flying bankers and other professionals. Both retain their Perth accents — among the clearer of those found north of the border — and both are excellent communicators. Brian is regularly asked to speak at conferences. He will turn up with two or three scraps of paper, his prompts, and hold an audience enthralled for up to an hour or more, often quoting detailed statistics from memory. As an after-dinner speaker, with an audience he knows, he is one of the funniest you could wish to hear, especially as he is always absolutely sober, and the likelihood is that most of those present have had several drinks (and some, perhaps, one too many!).

Stagecoach grew rapidly from the latter half of the 1980s. An executive team moved into acquired companies and decided very quickly who would or would not adapt to their very commercial approach to running buses. Some top managers departed more or less immediately, but many good people were found in acquired companies and went on to enjoy successful careers in Stagecoach.

Members of the executive team contributed all the necessary skills to re-shape acquired companies and to maximise profits. They grew in stature and experience as the Group grew and they oversaw heavy and regular investment in new vehicles. Further acquisitions saw some of them adapting their skills to working abroad and moving into other sectors of the transport industry, such as rail.

Stagecoach has now evolved into a large international transport organisation, with a turnover to the end of its 2003/4 financial year of nearly £1.8 billion. It is — and always has been — run as a tight ship. The base has always been in Perth. The current headquarters is a modest, modern building with around 35 corporate staff and another 65 or so in centralised functions like insurance and IT. The larger management offices face the rear of the building on the first floor, but Brian chose a smaller but still comfortable office at the front, overlooking one of the main roads into and out of Perth. He can break off in mid-sentence to observe the number of passengers on one of his passing buses, then pick up seamlessly to continue where he left off!

There is a refreshing informality about the whole operation. Everyone is addressed by his or her first name, as has happened since the earliest days. It is not familiarity, because it is courteous, but it indicates a first-class team spirit. That is why one of the first decisions, when writing this book, was to use first names for all the executive directors, while remaining more formal for the non-executives, or where there might be any confusion.

Brian and Ann signing for the acquisition of one of the NBC subsidiaries.

There is almost a family feel to the company, but it would be going too far to describe it as patriarchal. Stagecoach, wrongly, gained the reputation of being a hire-and-fire outfit, especially in its earlier years. Employee retention has always been one of the strengths of Stagecoach.

A recurring theme of this book is the way that Stagecoach — and that really means Brian — has been the first to predict the way that the industry is going. As he puts it: 'Stagecoach has been first over the trenches, the first to take the flak, and the first to secure the objective.' When he looks back on the business, he describes Stagecoach as having been a lovely youngster, a truculent teenager, and now mature — a very appropriate analogy.

In researching the story, I interviewed Ann, Brian, Ewan Brown, Graham Eccles, Martin Griffiths, Adrian Havlin, Neil Renilson, Derek Scott and Les Warneford. In addition I spoke to several other people in the industry who freely contributed their anecdotes and opinions. I am also grateful to Steven Stewart and Lynn Robertson, for giving me their time and arranging meetings. The phenomenal rate at which Stagecoach has grown means that it has sometimes been difficult to identify precise dates and other data; any errors, therefore, are mine, and I apologise for them here.

For the supply of photographs I should like to thank David Cole and others, notably Brian Morrison. Many of the earlier photographs came from a large box in the Stagecoach headquarters; although none had any copyright noted on it, I am grateful to those who took them and hope that they will be pleased to see their material used in this book.

Last, but by no means least, my thanks go to Chris Thompson, my secretary, for all her hard work.

Doug Jack
Ashby St Ledgers
(between United Counties and Midland Red South)
May 2005

The Volvo B10M with Alexander PS bodywork has proved to be a very reliable and durable bus and can be found in all Stagecoach fleets outside London. New in 1995, Midland Red South 209 (M209 LHP) is seen in Coventry the following June.

In its 25-year history Stagecoach has grown into a global transport provider. A recent delivery for its New Zealand bus operations is this prototype Designline low-floor trolleybus for the Wellington network.

The Age of the Stage

TIMING, location, ability and vision are all essential to creating a successful business. Perth is strategically located between the Highlands and Lowlands of Scotland. It promotes itself as the Perfect Centre. Sitting largely on one side of the River Tay, by 1980 it was declining in importance as a rail junction, but it was at the heart of a rapidly improving trunk-road network. Edinburgh lay just over 40 miles to the south, by motorway and the Forth Road Bridge. Much of the route to Glasgow was dual carriageway, with a short section of motorway. Grants of European money were transforming the tortuous old road to Inverness and the north of Scotland, while the route east to Dundee had become a dual carriageway, and the road thence to Aberdeen was being upgraded to the same standard.

To those of us who lived in the central belt of Scotland, Perth seemed a genteel place. But, like all Scottish towns and cities, it has its large postwar council housing estates. On one of these, Letham, Iain and Catherine Souter brought up their three children. Ann, their daughter, took up nursing, rising to become a theatre sister at Bridge of Earn Hospital, about four miles south of Perth; this had been built towards the end of World War 2, initially to treat injured servicemen, and had established a fine reputation in the region. David, their elder son, became a missionary in Africa, and later a Church of Scotland minister; he worked with Stagecoach from 1980 to 1987, but was never a shareholder. Brian, their younger son, was born in May 1954, 11½ years after Ann. Despite the gap in age, Brian and Ann have always been very close and have worked well together. Ewan Brown, later to play such an important role in the Stagecoach story, describes them as a remarkable partnership. They seemed to know instinctively who did what.

Iain Souter worked as a bus driver for W. Alexander & Sons Ltd, and later Alexander (Midland), at its Perth garage. He also drove taxis and hearses, and bought and sold cars to boost his income. His habits of working hard and the art of dealing passed to his family.

In 1976 Ann and her then husband, Robin Gloag, set up a business renting self-drive minibuses and motor caravans, called Gloagtrotter. The business grew steadily, because at that time far fewer people owned cars than do nowadays, but it depended heavily on the summer season. The next development was into public service vehicles. The first was a second-hand Ford Transit, bought from Strathmartine of Dundee in March 1980.

Brian had decided to become an accountant. He paid his way through his studies by working part-time as a bus conductor for Central SMT, mainly on routes between Glasgow and East Kilbride. It was hard work, combining his shifts with classes and studies at Strathclyde University, but he succeeded, passing his final year with distinction, and was taken on by Arthur Andersen for the three-year apprenticeship that enabled him to qualify as a Chartered Accountant.

Central SMT was strongly unionised, and there were frequent disputes. Brian became a member of the union and learned a lot about management-employee relationships. His time with Central SMT also gave him first-hand experience of two types of buses that were to figure quite prominently in the first 10 years of the Stagecoach story. Most of the double-deckers were Bristol Lodekkas, while the single-deckers for local services were mainly Leyland Leopards with Alexander Y-type bodywork. Both were solid, reliable models.

Working with Arthur Andersen was excellent training. Young accountants were often sent to clients to carry out detailed work on annual audits, but Brian was uncomfortable, quite literally, with the formal dress code of suits and ties! Derek Scott, another leading light in the Stagecoach story, had joined Arthur Andersen two years before Brian and worked with him on a number of audits. The normal practice was to sit at a spare desk with the client's own accounting staff, but Brian was sometimes unconventional. He would frequently talk to other employees to get a feel for how the client was performing. On one occasion, cleaners told him that the factory he was auditing was about to be closed down. The management had not yet told the auditors, but his information turned out to be correct.

Soon after qualifying, Brian left Arthur Andersen to join Ann and Robin in their growing business, but he remained on good terms with the firm. However, like all the major accountancy groups, it would not normally offer to work for clients who had less than a certain minimum annual turnover, and while the senior partners were aware of Brian's interest in operating buses and coaches they must have been surprised — and impressed — when the fledgling business soon needed their services. The rapidly growing company started to have issues with banks, moving through three of them quite quickly, and for one of those changes Derek Scott, who had kept in contact with Brian, prepared a financial report to the end of December 1982 on its first two years of trading. Stagecoach later engaged Arthur Andersen as its auditor for many years and, as it grew, recruited several of the firm's senior executives. Ultimately, however, the major international accountancy group was fatally wounded by its involvement in the Enron *débâcle*, and Brian must be bemused now to ponder that Stagecoach has survived his former employer!

In his new career, one of Brian's first priorities was to obtain a PSV driver's licence, borrowing an old Daimler double-decker — one of the rare ones with a manual gearbox — from A. & C. McLennan, then a sizeable independent operator in Perth. By passing his test on a double-decker with a manual gearbox, he was then permitted to drive any other kind of public service vehicle.

The GT Coaches partnership between Brian, Ann and Robin was formed in March 1980 and, very soon afterwards, bought its first full-size bus, an elderly

Bristol MW5G with 45-seat ECW bodywork, which had been new to the Bristol Omnibus Co. They soon secured a contract to carry workers north from Perth to one of the major improvement projects on the A9 road. Within three weeks they had recovered the cost of the bus. By this time Iain Souter had been made redundant by Alexander (Midland), and he put his redundancy money into the growing business. A further three used coaches were bought, and the partnership moved to premises in Friarton Road, by Perth harbour. Work comprised a mixture of private hires and contracts.

Traditionally the bus and coach industry in the United Kingdom had been tightly regulated: operators had to obtain a licence for each and every route, specifying the termini, roads used, stops, timetables and fare structures. This applied not only to local routes, but also to long-distance services, excursions and tours. This system had been established by the Road Traffic Act 1930, mainly to protect the railways from growing competition from bus and haulage companies. Any application for a new licence had to be made to the Traffic Commissioner for the area in which the applicant was based. It was very hard for newcomers to the industry to obtain a licence, because the established operators and British Rail could (and frequently did) object; if they could demonstrate that there was likely to be abstraction of passengers from their services, the new application almost inevitably failed.

Bus and express-coach services were controlled almost entirely by the public sector. London Transport had a very tight grip on its area, while Passenger Transport Executives (PTEs) controlled operations in seven major conurbations — the West Midlands, Merseyside, Greater Manchester, South Yorkshire, West Yorkshire, Tyne & Wear and Strathclyde — and there were just under 50 municipally owned operators in various other towns and cities. The National Bus Company, through its subsidiaries, operated many of the other routes in England and Wales, including serving cities as large as Bristol and Oxford. The subsidiaries of Scottish Bus Group ran almost all the services outside the four largest cities in Scotland. Ulsterbus had practically a monopoly in Northern Ireland. A number of independent operators had local service licences, mostly in more rural areas.

Throughout the 1970s operators had enjoyed a subsidy of 50% of the purchase price of new vehicles used on local services, known as New Bus Grant. They had to comply with certain design features, including the facility for the driver to collect fares, known as one-man operation. Under this initiative, the average ages of most fleets had steadily declined during the decade and operators were, in some cases, replacing buses well before they were time-expired.

In May 1979 Margaret Thatcher and the Conservative Party came to power. As well as reducing Bus Grant by 10% per annum from 1980 to 1984 the Conservatives — great believers in free market forces — also started to make fundamental changes to the way that the operating industry worked. Under the Transport Act 1980, all services of more than 30 miles in length were freed from regulation. Operators no longer had to apply to the Traffic Commissioner for a licence; instead, they had only to give 42 days' notice of their intention to start a service, including the route and timetable. The new system became effective from 6 October 1980.

The subsidiaries of the Scottish Bus Group and the National Bus Company had extensive networks of express services. Their strength lay in strong national networks of ticketing agents. Their weakness was the relatively poor standard of their coaches, with few comforts for passengers on long journeys like Scotland to London, partly because many were bought with a view to being cascaded to more local work in later life.

Right from the earliest days, Brian had a talent for strategic thinking. He could see that an operator who got in at the very start of deregulation of longer-distance services could build a business, and persuaded Ann and Robin to move into long-distance express services. The first two coaches, bought second-hand for that purpose, were a Volvo B58 and an AEC Reliance.

The partnership was quick off the mark, starting an overnight service from Dundee to London on 9 October 1980. David Souter, the second driver, passed his PSV driving test only that morning. Coaches called at Perth, Stirling, Cumbernauld and Glasgow, with fares under-cutting those of the Scottish Bus Group. The single fare from Dundee to London was £9.50, and from Glasgow to London £6.75. Southbound journeys

A typical view from the early days of Stagecoach operations, showing the original style of application of the company's fleet name. This must have been one of the first applications of the tan, red and blue bands, before the vertical stripes were reversed above the waist rail to form an arrowhead. HDV 639E was a Bristol MW6G with 39-seat Eastern Coach Works body, dating from 1967. It is still owned, as part of the heritage fleet.

The first colour scheme used by GT Coaches, seen here on the 1967 Bristol MW6G/ECW on a snowy day in Perth.

ran on Thursday, Friday, Saturday and Sunday nights, returning from London one day later.

Large numbers of passengers were soon being carried and, from quite an early date, extra coaches had to be hired. From 26 January 1981 the London route was extended northwards to Aberdeen, and twice-daily journeys were introduced between Aberdeen and Glasgow. The inland road, bypassing Brechin and Forfar, was being upgraded as the main route between Aberdeen and Dundee, but Stagecoach followed the coast, serving towns like Montrose and Arbroath.

David Souter was responsible for the company's marketing, including timetables. He came up with the name Stagecoach, used on all the company's publicity material and, very soon afterwards, on the long-distance express vehicles. It was a brilliant name, because it was so easy for passengers to remember, and that far outweighed the downside of carping from competitors about a cowboy outfit.

The Scottish Bus Group was using a variety of coaches on its express services from Edinburgh and Glasgow to London, all with Alexander M-type bodywork. Although they had reclining seats and a toilet they were not particularly comfortable. Their distinguishing feature was the use of a higher waistrail with small, forward-sloping side windows, similar to those on Greyhound coaches in the USA, the idea being that passengers on overnight services did not need a large expanse of glass.

Volvo had come into the top end of the British coach market, introducing higher power and air-over-leaf suspension on its B58. That model had a wonderful reputation for reliability and quickly became a favourite with Stagecoach. By 1980 it was well known that Leyland was developing the Tiger to replace the Leopard and AEC Reliance and that Volvo would replace the B58 with the B10M. The Scottish Bus Group placed orders for B10M and Tiger coaches to update its London fleet and meet the new competition.

Duple, at the time one of the two main coach-builders in Britain, developed additional variants of the Dominant body range, including the Dominant III, with the same style of small, sloping side windows, and secured an initial order for 16 from SBG. The design was not exclusive to SBG, however, and a number were ordered by dealers on other makes of chassis, including Stanley Hughes of Leeds, on Volvo B58 and B10M chassis.

Duple launched its new Dominant III and Dominant IV models at a series of regional road shows, including one at its depot at Barrhead, just outside Glasgow. To help his customers Kevin Wood, then Duple's Marketing Manager (and now Coach Sales Director at Plaxton) introduced a range of paint layouts, called Stylelines, including a striped scheme which Stagecoach specified in tan, red and blue on a white background. Ann went with Brian to look at the new coaches, having collected him from an overnight service from London. They looked like they couldn't rub two pennies together, but one of the sales staff introduced them to Mel McGrath of Stanley Hughes, with whom they subsequently enjoyed a good relationship for several years.

Because of chassis delivery schedules, some of the dealer-stock Dominant IIIs were built before the SBG orders, and one was bought by Stagecoach in February 1981, becoming its first ever brand-new vehicle. It had 50 very comfortable fixed seats and a rear-mounted toilet. Senior executives at SBG, already dismissive of the upstarts from Perth, were really peeved that Stagecoach was the first to put the new design into service and had some harsh words for Duple! The new coach went on to cover 1 million miles in little over three years, then ran a further 500,000 miles on express services within Scotland, eventually accumulating around 2 million miles before being retired and preserved by Stagecoach.

In December 1980 Stagecoach acquired its first local stage-carriage service, taking over A. & C. McLennan's route from Perth to Errol (approximately halfway to Dundee). This came with a depot at Errol, giving more space for maintenance.

In February 1981 a further overnight service was introduced between Aberdeen and Newcastle-upon-Tyne, running through Perth, Edinburgh and Berwick-on-Tweed. The principal attraction at Newcastle was the newly opened Metro Centre, one of the largest indoor shopping centres in Europe. However, it failed to attract sufficient customers from Scotland, so after three months the service was cut back to Edinburgh, running during daytime.

Competition on the express journeys was coming from several new directions, in addition to the established SBG services. Cotters, which ran a small but high-quality extended-tours business in Glasgow, bought eight high-specification Volvo/Van Hool coaches — featuring two compartments, each with 20 reclining seats, separated by a central galley — and charged a premium for the higher level of service on its Glasgow–London service.

Park's of Hamilton was competing on the Glasgow–London route and also, for several months, between Glasgow and Aberdeen. Park's opened a coach station in Glasgow that was used by most of the independent operators, including its competitors. A shrewd character, Douglas Park had taken on a small traditional family coach firm as a 21-year-old in 1971. He rapidly became the largest independent coach operator in Scotland, building up a good mix of work for his modern fleet. He was probably the first to realise that there was too much competition on express services, and that Stagecoach had not only built a very strong brand in a short space of time but also had the most efficient booking and scheduling systems. Consequently he withdrew his own London services and started providing coaches for Stagecoach, in his own company's colours but carrying boards on each side with the Stagecoach name.

A contrast in coach styling at the City Coach Station in Glasgow with a Bristol MW6G alongside one of the very impressive Super Stagecoach Neoplan Skyliner double-deckers.

Service frequencies to and from London were stepped up to daily from March 1981, and for the summer season a new route was introduced between Aberdeen and Blackpool, the single fare being £11.50. To meet the increased demand a further four new Volvo B10M/Duple coaches were bought. While most major fleets wrote down full-size buses and coaches over 15 years, Brian recognised that Stagecoach was sweating its assets and, almost from the beginning, wrote coaches down at 15% per annum, or 6.67 years.

Further competition came when Newton of Dingwall and Allander of Milngavie started running services from Edinburgh and Glasgow through Perth to Inverness. Then came the first of many appearances before the authorities. Stagecoach wanted to convert the licence for the Glasgow–Aberdeen service from express to limited-stop stage-carriage, with additional stops on the route, which would have enabled the company to claim a rebate of 80% of the duty on fuel. Objections were lodged with the Traffic Commissioner by British Rail, Alexander (Midland), Alexander (Northern) and three regional councils. The Commissioner granted the application, but the objectors immediately lodged an appeal with the Secretary of State for Transport. He subsequently upheld the appeal, obliging Stagecoach to revert to express operation. Brian then tried to have this decision overturned in the Court of Session (Scotland's High Court), but without success.

Early in 1982 the partners decided to concentrate fully on bus and coach operations and therefore sold the motor-caravan and minibus-hire operations. This gave them further capital, and it was boosted by an investment of £25,000 by Ann's and Brian's uncle, Fraser McColl, the president of a large Canadian company, who became a mentor to his nephew and niece. At that time Brian did all the accounting and the payroll, and he recalls taking the books with him on the flight to Canada and preparing the Profit & Loss Account and the Balance Sheet over the Atlantic.

Brian took what he describes as the biggest gamble of his career when he persuaded his partners to buy two Neoplan Skyliner double-deck coaches, which arrived in April and May 1982. Costing around £100,000 each, the Skyliners were dramatically styled, with 77 reclining seats and on-board toilet and galley facilities. Brian calls them 'gobsmackingly good-looking' vehicles that were properly designed for long-distance work. Built to the Continental overall maximum height limit of 4m (or a shade over 13ft), they had independent front suspension, so the height of the floor in the lower deck was around 350mm above the ground. The main entrance was just ahead of the rear axle, with a staircase to the upper deck, and a large walk-in luggage locker was located over the two rear axles, helping to insulate the noise from the rear-mounted engine. Brian reckons that their centre of gravity, when laden, was little different from that of a high-floor single-deck coach.

When painting the Skyliners Neoplan used basic-ally the same scheme as had Duple, but with deeper horizontal bands, then reversed the three broader forward-sloping bands, so that they sloped rearward over the inter-deck side panels towards the roof. This, with minor variations, would be the Stagecoach house style for the best part of 20 years.

Some of the Skyliners were marketed by Stagecoach as the Super Stage, running an additional direct route between Aberdeen, Birmingham and London, avoid-

ing Glasgow. On-board meals were served, using Zanussi hot-boxes, and videos were also included in the very competitive fare of £15 single or £26 return. Curiously the fares to Birmingham and London were the same. Meals — and sandwiches for other services — were prepared by a team of ladies led by Catherine Souter.

The investment in the Neoplans proved to be a shrewd move, because they practically doubled the number of permutations available when scheduling services and duplicates. Services started with a 50-seat coach, and, as further bookings came in, especially on busy days, seating capacity could be increased progressively to one 77-seat Neoplan, two 50-seat coaches, a 50-seat coach and one Neoplan, two Neoplans, and so on. Drivers' wages were a major element in the operating costs. By being capable of carrying 50% more passengers at the same wage costs, the Neoplans proved their worth so quickly that a further pair joined the fleet before the end of 1982. Visiting London one day in 1983, the late Albrecht Auwärter, then Chief Executive of Neoplan, went to have a look at two of his coaches and simply could not believe the mileage that they had already accumulated, especially when he was reminded that a mile was around 1.6km!

Also joining the fleet, for contract work, were much more humble double-deckers in the shape of Bristol

Top: Deregulation of express coach services in the UK started on 6 October 1980. Three days later, Stagecoach started running between Dundee and London. One of the first coaches was this AEC Reliance with Plaxton bodywork and 57 fixed seats; travel rugs were provided for additional comfort. This was the first application of the Stagecoach name, but as two words.

Above: FES 831W was the very first coach bought new by Stagecoach. It was a Volvo B58-61 with Duple Dominant III coachwork, seating 50 on deep, fixed seats that were remarkably comfortable. The small main side windows were double-glazed — a considerable benefit on overnight travel. It was parked in the sunshine outside the premises in Friarton Road, Perth.

Top: This Neoplan Skyliner carried Stagecoach names but was initially in non-corporate colours, having been supplied from dealer stock.

Above: A view from the early days of Stagecoach, showing a short Bristol Lodekka (FS) with an open rear platform in an interim livery, and a freshly repainted forward-entrance FLF model on the left, in what would become the corporate standard.

Below: A busy scene in the booking office in the early days of Stagecoach. Almost all contact with customers, and with drivers on the road, was by telephone. A young Brian is seen on the right-hand side of the picture.

Lodekkas (three of which, incidentally, came from Central SMT), which Stagecoach preferred to early rear-engined double-deckers that were also available on the second-hand market. The Lodekka had been the first model to go into volume production in the UK with the floor in the lower deck only one step above the ground, five decades before that layout was to become mandatory; it was also the first design to offer two central gangways within a height of just over 13ft, meaning that Lodekkas could pass safely under most of the low bridges in the Perth area. Despite requiring a crew of two, minders being carried on school services and conductresses on the country routes, the Lodekka was also a real accountant's bus: although not the easiest of vehicles to drive if fitted with Bristol's own manual gearbox, its six-cylinder Gardner engine was renowned for fuel economy; Brian recalls fondly that his examples returned up to 14mpg and cost (at mid-1980s prices) about 4p per mile to maintain.

Any new business needs a little bit of luck, and for Stagecoach this came in July 1982, when British Rail was shut down by a prolonged strike. Such was the demand that Stagecoach had to hire in coaches from other operators, especially for the express services within Scotland, and several weeks of very heavy loadings gave a valuable boost to income.

From March 1983 Stagecoach served Inverness, from where (via Perth) daily services were provided to Glasgow, and an overnight service to London. An interesting feature of the operation was the use of an interchange point at Canal Street, Perth, where there was a meeting with the southbound coach from Aberdeen; if loadings were light, passengers could be consolidated in one vehicle for the rest of the journey.

It is fascinating to talk to Brian about these early days — and to reflect on the enormous advances in communications in the last 20 years. When Stagecoach started its express services all contact with customers — and drivers all around the country — was by telephone. From a fairly early date there were eight lines on the switchboard, staffed by a team of women who took all the bookings. There was a strong internal discipline that all telephone calls had to be answered as quickly as possible. Sometime later, landlines were established from London and Glasgow, meaning that passengers could book from those cities at local call rates. It was expensive for Stagecoach, but generated valuable additional business.

Brian set up a system very like that nowadays used by the low-cost airlines. Passengers were given a reference that entitled them to travel on their chosen day and departure time. They were not allocated seat numbers. Most bookings were made a week or two before the day of travel, but in the holiday period this was often extended to six weeks or so ahead. Most payments were by cheque or postal order. The strategy was always to run each coach as full as possible. Sometimes seats were oversold, as with the airlines, and the company very occasionally paid passengers to delay their travel to the next journey.

At busy times Brian would watch how bookings were coming in and allocate coaches accordingly, not confirming the routeings of duplicate vehicles until the morning of departure, when passenger lists were drawn up manually and the numbers and sizes of vehicles arranged to allow for a few last-minute sales. On a typical day a driver would take a coach north to Aberdeen, and either he or his conductress would phone in before the southbound departure, to be advised of any last-minute bookings. Conductresses collected fares from last-minute passengers and, when two or more vehicles were travelling in convoy, changed from coach to coach in a convenient layby, such that they were on their feet practically all the way, from Aberdeen through Dundee to Perth. Conductresses could also change direction, selling fares to southbound passengers as far south as Hamilton or as far north as Cumbernauld before changing coach to return to Glasgow. Glasgow was the best point for last-minute sales.

Tuesdays and Wednesdays were the quietest days on express services, so that was when the company concentrated on regular maintenance of vehicles that were achieving very high mileages. The busiest day of the week for southbound journeys was normally Friday, and the busiest for returns was Sunday. Friday afternoons became the critical time, with engineering staff driving school buses and thereby relieving their normal drivers to work on duplicates. If it really came to the crunch, Brian had a PSV licence, but he would be reluctant to leave the office during such a busy period. The pressure eased somewhat from 6pm, when part-time drivers — needed to meet any last-minute surge in loadings and to relieve full-time drivers before they ran out of hours — started to come in. The peak demand for express services on Fridays also meant a re-shuffling of the fleet; every single-deck coach was allocated to express services, including duplicates, and the old double-deckers took over all the school runs and local services. The northbound peak on Sundays was not so critical, there being, of course, no school contracts.

Early in 1983 Ann's and Robin's marriage broke up. Soon afterwards Robin left the partnership, taking one coach and some schools and works contracts, and started to trade from a base at Errol under the 'Highwayman' name. At around the same time Stagecoach's registered office and booking facilities moved from Friarton Road to a three-storey house at 24 Marshall Place, overlooking Perth's South Inch.

In April 1983 Stagecoach Ltd, which had been formed as a limited company two years earlier to enter into leasing agreements, took over the former Gloagtrotter/GT Coaches partnership, this change in status being requested by the bankers at that time. It was purely structural for financial planning and was not noticed by passengers who were already familiar with the Stagecoach name.

Although happy with the Neoplan Skyliners, Stagecoach next turned to Van Hool for three of their integral Astromega double-deck coaches. These were specified with a bus-type double-width front entrance opposite the driver and thus qualified for Bus Grant of 30% of the purchase price, being bought when the Aberdeen–Glasgow service was run as a limited-stop service, but to Brian's annoyance the grant had to be repaid when the service was forced to revert to express operation. The Van Hool double-deckers did not stand up well to the intensity of Stagecoach's services. The luggage compartment was over the rear-mounted engine and became so hot that some of the cheap plastic luggage then fashionable started to melt on long journeys. All three needed quite extensive re-working by the Belgian manufacturer in the autumn of 1983. Each coach was off the road for three weeks, so Brian put in a claim for hiring in a replacement vehicle for nine weeks at £300 per week.

Van Hool refused to meet that claim, but it was eventually settled, as we shall see, many years later.

At the end of August 1983 a new route was introduced between Edinburgh and Glasgow. There were 12 journeys in each direction, between Waverley Bridge, Edinburgh, and Park's City Coach Station in Glasgow, and in order to support these Stagecoach leased a small depot and workshop at North Canal Bank Street, just north of Glasgow's city centre. Although Stagecoach undercut the SBG fares on this busy corridor, the state-owned company not only retaliated, by bringing fares down to the same level, but also increased its frequency to every half hour. A few years later Stagecoach ran into a period of skirmishes with the Office of Fair Trading and the Monopolies & Mergers Commission, the company frequently being accused of predatory action against competitors. Brian says that, in 1983, he was not even aware of the OFT, but that, if he had been, SBG's action on the Glasgow–Edinburgh services would have warranted an appeal.

The travelling public in Scotland were the main beneficiaries of the competition created by the Transport Act 1980. Not only were there several operators on the same route; there were also higher frequencies, lower fares and much more modern vehicles, with features like reclining seats, double glazing, soft trim, improved heating/ventilation systems and the provision of toilets combining to make coach travel significantly more comfortable.

The strong competition on coach services continued when Cotters started running twice daily between Aberdeen, Dundee, Perth and London. Stagecoach had by that time become very well established in Aberdeen and Dundee and retained the loyalty of the vast majority of regular passengers. Brian suspects that the people who defected were those who realised that competitors' coaches were more lightly loaded and therefore offered them a greater likelihood of being able to spread out on a double seat.

Many of Stagecoach's express vehicles were working very high mileages. They were fortunate in that most of the motorway network was nothing like as congested as it is nowadays and that high average speeds could be maintained; moreover, at that time coaches were still permitted to use the outside lane.

Stagecoach expanded rapidly in the latter half of 1983. In November it acquired Adamson & Low, which traded in Edinburgh as Adamson Coaches; this

The busy scene in Aberdeen in 1983. One of the three Van Hool Astromegas heads a line-up that includes three Neoplan Skyliners, suggesting that this might well have been taken at a busy summer weekend. Passing on the left is a Leyland Atlantean of Grampian Regional Transport, followed by a Northern Scottish bus.

The Volvo B58 soon came to be favoured by the expanding Stagecoach for second-hand acquisitions, because of its reliability and durability. This example had Duple Dominant II Express bodywork and had been freshly painted in corporate colours. The photograph must have been taken soon after the operations at Perth moved to Walnut Grove, close to the River Tay.

added a further 17 vehicles to the fleet, most being used on contract work in and around Scotland's capital. In December the service operated by Bennett of Kilwinning from Ardrossan to Glasgow was taken over, together with two nearly new Leyland Leopard coaches. New vehicles comprised another three Neoplan Skyliners, along with seven more Volvo B10Ms, three with Duple bodies and four with Plaxton, the three Van Hool Astromegas being traded in for the Plaxton-bodied Volvos. Including a number of used acquisitions, the total fleet strength now amounted to nearly 50 vehicles.

Towards the end of the year the company moved its offices and depot to a much more spacious facility at Walnut Grove, just outside Perth on the road towards Dundee. Derek Scott remembers Walnut Grove as a hive of activity; coaches full of passengers would regularly drive round to the rear of the depot, where they were not only refuelled but frequently also had their toilets dumped! He often wondered if many of the passengers were aware of what was happening. On the subject of toilets, Ann recalls that those on the Duple coaches occasionally leaked chemical fluid into the luggage compartment below. One particular lady from Perth had won a national competition held by the Avon cosmetics company and had bought a posh frock in the most expensive shop in Perth to go to an awards ceremony in London. She took the coach overnight and Ann received an irate phone call the following morning about a very unpleasant fragrance in her suitcase. All she could do was apologise and invite the lady to buy a replacement dress at Stagecoach's expense.

In the early years nobody was on duty overnight, Brian and Ann arranging to have calls diverted from the switchboard to their homes on alternate nights. If they were lucky, they got a complete night's sleep. London coaches made a half-hour stop in the middle of the night at Charnock Richard service area, and sometimes passengers went into the café, dozed off, missed the coach and then phoned to complain. Occasionally, however, there would be a major incident. One night there was a big pile-up, involving

several coaches, on the M6 motorway. Brian and Ann had to transfer the night line to the offices and were there for the next 24 hours, dealing with anxious passengers, relatives and lost luggage. On another night one of the Neoplans caught fire, fortunately without any loss of life or serious injury, but many passengers lost their suitcases, and then the claims started to come in. Ann wonders to this day why anyone should have had more than one gold chain in his/her case! By contrast, when some people lost their property the last thing they wanted was to get it back. Ann remembered a lady who said that her son had lost, amongst other items, a pair of white leather shoes and a cashmere jersey. The case, with a pair of white sandals and a tatty pullover, was subsequently found. Ann could hardly stop laughing when she recounted telephoning the said lady and asking whether these were the items that she was looking for!

With hindsight it is amazing that, during this period of rapid expansion, Stagecoach did not overheat. That was down to some very shrewd management and a lot of hard work. Brian was responsible for the financial control of the company, but Ann developed a fearsome reputation as an extremely tough purchaser. While she was rapidly learning about the business, she frequently compared notes with Douglas Park about parts and fuel prices. He, like Ann, was a tough negotiator and knew instinctively just how far to push.

The purchase of diesel was a major item in the monthly expenditure, and Ann would ring round the various fuel companies to see which was offering the best terms. She recalls being pestered regularly by a very nervous Englishman who worked for Shell and who kept calling into the office to collect the cheque for each month's fuel. Somewhat exasperated by this, Brian decided to pay him in cash. All the money that had come from local services was added up, put in a large crate and loaded by a couple of strong employees into the boot of his car. Despite his protests, Brian reassured him that there was nothing better than cash and sent him on his way. He never troubled Brian or Ann again, and it also saved the bank charges for counting a large quantity of cash!

Stagecoach relied very heavily on manufacturers for parts and service support — one of the reasons Volvo became the main choice of single-deck coach; it was not the most economical vehicle, but its reliability and durability stood up to the company's punishing schedules. When an engine seized on one of the early B10M coaches Sandy Glennie, then

The Stagecoach office at the City Coach Station in Glasgow with prominent advertising for all the various services, including those to the Ayrshire coast, acquired from Bennetts of Kilwinning.

General Manager of Volvo Bus (UK), gave Stagecoach the benefit of the doubt and accepted it as a warranty item. That certainly helped to seal the relationship.

Hans Martin Maier, at that time Neoplan's charismatic Export Director, had no doubt as to who was his most demanding customer. When one of the Skyliners was off the road he arranged for a vital part to be air-freighted from Stuttgart to Edinburgh in a matter of hours — and this at a time when there were fewer flights than there are today, with no direct link between the two cities. When the phone rang again from Perth he expected praise for his efforts, only to be told: 'I was a hospital sister, and we never left anyone lying on a table for eight hours waiting for parts!'

In the first few months SBG executives were fond of predicting that Stagecoach was a bubble that was liable to burst at any moment. They regularly had their staff monitoring Stagecoach vehicles and compiling records of where and when they had been seen, and these were collated into Board reports. Senior executives found it very hard to believe the mileages that were being achieved.

Sometimes there was a more sinister side to SBG's activities, whereby inspectors would approach a queue of waiting Stagecoach passengers, telling them that their coach had broken down and would not turn up. However, as most people had already paid for their seats, this tactic rarely worked.

As Stagecoach consolidated SBG began to take the company more seriously. Evidence of this came when the company applied to turn its service between Edinburgh and Inverness into a stage-carriage operation. Before the application reached the Traffic Commissioners Stagecoach met and negotiated with three SBG subsidiaries and two regional councils. Objections were withdrawn once Stagecoach agreed not to carry passengers between Edinburgh and Dunfermline.

Although there was strong competition, operators had their trade association, at that time the Bus & Coach Council (and nowadays the Confederation of Passenger Transport), where they met and discussed issues that were of common interest. Ann and Brian, both very good at communication and negotiation, soon joined, attending the annual conference at Gleneagles from around 1983. At first they sat in a corner, but they made themselves known and soon became widely accepted, especially as the Government's plans unfolded. They predicted that the level of competition on express coach services could not continue but made it clear that they intended to be among the survivors. On one occasion Brian met Ian Irwin, Chairman of the Scottish Transport Group, and told him that his ambition was to run all the buses in Scotland! At another Gleneagles conference they had been shown into the hospitality lounge for the top table and only when being piped into the banqueting hall realised that they should have been sitting at one of the ordinary tables!

In response to the new competition from the private sector the National Bus Company subsidiaries had introduced the powerful National Express brand and had bought many new coaches, and, quite soon thereafter, a number of their competitors retired from the scene south of the border. Others, like Trathens of Plymouth, stopped running their own services and began to operate on contract to National Express. Similarly, SBG had introduced the Scottish Citylink brand, and all coaches were painted in the same livery.

Brian stands in front of one of the first of many former London Routemasters bought by Stagecoach over the years.

In the early 1980s the Government was assessing the results of deregulation of coach services and planning the next stage of its strategy for the bus industry. It came to the conclusion that not enough competition had been created, ignoring the fact that coaches also had competition from cars, trains, and, over longer distances, from airlines.

Early in 1984 the Government published a White Paper that formed the basis of the Transport Act 1985. All local bus services, except in London and Northern Ireland, would be deregulated with effect from October 1986. The National Bus Company was to be broken down into a large number of small units and privatised. Management teams were encouraged to bid for their companies by being offered reimbursement of the fees of advisers and a 5% discount. Prospective purchasers could not make offers for subsidiaries with contiguous operating territories and were limited to a maximum of three bids. The Transport Minister at the time, Nicholas Ridley, had a vision of thousands of drivers, each owning one or two buses, all over the country. That was never going to work. Instead, his Act was a major opportunity for public-sector managers who were willing to take the risk of owning and running their own companies, and for entrepreneurial newcomers like Stagecoach.

Brian studied the Transport Act very closely and started to develop the next stage of Stagecoach's strategy. The express-coach business was seasonal. Brian always liked stage-carriage operation, because it normally brought in regular income all year round.

There were two strategies available to Stagecoach. The first was to try going into competition with existing operators by developing innovative services. The second was to grow by taking part in the NBC privatisation and acquiring some of its subsidiaries. The latter was a very ambitious plan, so Brian set about maximising profits from the existing services; he knew that he would need a strong balance sheet and would have to mortgage Stagecoach to get in on the NBC privatisation. As part of this process, Stagecoach withdrew from the Edinburgh–Glasgow route, because of intense competition from SBG and British Rail.

Brian's preparations for taking a role in the bus industry took a surprising turn in January 1985, when

Owned originally by A. & C. McLennan of Perth, this 1951 Leyland Tiger PS1/1 was acquired by Stagecoach and restored to its original colours, with the addition of the Bluebird motif. It is seen here with Brian in the foreground promoting heritage tours in Perthshire. The unusual angled window above the engine cover was to facilitate one-man operation.

Below left: In the 1980s old buses were withdrawn and stored in the extensive former McLennan depot at Spittalfield, north of Perth. This Bristol Lodekka had already donated a headlight to another bus and would gradually be stripped of all reusable parts.

Below right: Northern General Transport had bought a fleet of Routemasters with forward entrances and Leyland engines. One of these subsequently found its way to Stagecoach and is seen in the yard at Spittalfield.

five former London Transport AEC Routemasters arrived at Perth. These vehicles had an excellent reputation for reliability, even in the arduous traffic conditions in London. Because of the front-engine layout and open rear platform they needed a driver and conductress. While that increased the running costs, point-to-point journey times were considerably quicker, and the conductress could help passengers on and off, in addition to collecting fares. The first Routemaster started running between Perth and Errol a couple of months later, and then, in May, another five arrived, running on local contract services in the Perth area.

The next innovation, in March 1985, was an attempt to amend the express-service licences between Scotland and London so that passengers could be picked up and set down at every motorway service area. (At the time these were not as numerous as they are now.) All the service-area operators gave consent except Blue Boar, which had the franchise to run Watford Gap and Rothersthorpe in Northamptonshire. However, the Department of Transport was unwilling to accept the idea, stating that service areas were not bus stops. Undaunted, Stagecoach lodged

an application with the Metropolitan Traffic Commissioner to pick up and set down passengers at Scratchwood service area at the southern end of the M1. Although there were no objections, the Commissioner reviewed the case and came to the conclusion that the proposals not only fell foul of the Highways Act 1980 but also would be of minimal benefit to the travelling public. Had the application been granted, Stagecoach would have been able to claim fuel-duty rebate.

After several months managing Park's City Coach Station in Glasgow, Stagecoach took control in June 1985. In November of that year, Stagecoach took over all the services and vehicles from the trustees of A. & C. McLennan of Perth, including a depot with a large amount of land at Spittalfield, about 12 miles north of Perth. McLennan ran several rural routes, connecting Perth, Dunkeld and Blairgowrie, and also some contract services.

Deregulation of local bus services took effect from 26 October 1986. For several months before that operators were busy registering those services that they intended to retain after that date. Stagecoach applied for a triangle of services from Perth to

This Routemaster, working for Magicbus in Glasgow, appears to have had too thin a repaint into Stagecoach colours and could have done with another coat, to judge from the amount of London red showing through in various places. They were popular with passengers, because they offered rapid connections between the city centre and the huge Easterhouse housing estate.

Pitlochry, Perth to Aberfeldy and between Pitlochry and Aberfeldy. All had previously been operated by SBG subsidiary Strathtay Scottish, which did not register to run them after 26 October. In fact Stagecoach operated technically 'on hire' to Strathtay from 18 August. It probably did not appear that way at the time, but it was the start of the erosion of Strathtay's position in Perth by Stagecoach.

A much more significant development was the decision to operate three routes in Glasgow. Brian knew the city well from his days as a student and with Arthur Andersen and always viewed it as good bus-operating territory. Two services started from Buchanan Street bus station. The 18 ran to East Kilbride via Burnside, the 19 ran to the large Easterhouse estate using the M8 motorway, and the 20 connected St Enoch's Square and Castlemilk via Aikenhead Road. The most innovative of these was the 19, offering a much faster link between the city centre and Easterhouse.

A new subsidiary company, Magicbus (Scotland) Ltd, was formed, with its registered office at the North Canal Bank Street garage in Port Dundas. Services were started with 14 Routemasters, two Lodekkas and five Volvo B58 coaches. The use of the Magicbus name was another inspired choice and evidence of how Stagecoach kept in touch with its travelling public, 'Magic!' being widely used in Glasgow as an expression of satisfaction. The company also introduced innovative marketing, for instance the Magic Bunny (in a white rabbit suit) that would hop from bus to bus, to and from the city centre, handing out trinkets and sweets to children travelling with adults.

Strathclyde Buses was not at all happy about Magicbus's trying to run a competing service from St Enoch's Square and blocked off access to the first bus by a row of cones. Brian tried to remove them but was thwarted by some Strathclyde inspectors, so he used a megaphone to attract passengers to a temporary new terminus, just around the corner, and the Castlemilk service got off to an excellent start.

The London services continued to enjoy good patronage. For the winter of 1986/7 there was a daily daytime journey from Aberdeen via Glasgow and Manchester and an overnight journey from Aberdeen

via Birmingham. Each night there was also a service from Inverness via Perth, Edinburgh and Birmingham, and a daytime service at weekends from Inverness via Manchester. The Inverness and Aberdeen services met at Perth and could be consolidated if loadings were light, as sometimes happened in midweek.

The Magicbus services in Glasgow became profitable within three months, proving to Brian that it was possible to start competitive services, but they had required an enormous amount of management time. He came to the conclusion that it was better to buy bus companies than to compete and try to knock them out of the market. He knew there would be difficulties raising funds for his ambitious plans and therefore decided to make another visit to Fraser McColl in Canada. Fraser must have been impressed by the strategy, because he put up £800,000 in bank guarantees. Standard Chartered Bank was willing to back Stagecoach, and that enabled Brian and Ann to become involved in the NBC privatisation programme.

In 1986 Stagecoach acquired four DAF MB230 coaches with Duple 320 coachwork. C895 CSN rests between duties at Walnut Grove.

From Coaches to Buses

THE Conservative Government's plans to sell public-sector bus companies, especially the subsidiaries of the National Bus Company, had been common knowledge since the publication of draft legislation in 1984. With its large majority in Parliament, there was never any doubt that it would implement its policy. There was, however, a delay of several months while various advisers were appointed by the Department of Transport and while some of the subsidiaries were restructured in preparation for sale.

Eventually the NBC sale involved 58 bus fleets in England and Wales, nine engineering subsidiaries, Voyage National, based in Lille, France, with six coaches, National Holidays, National Travelworld (a travel agency), Victoria Coach Station and National Express. This last-named had only four coaches of its own but ran a network of services that required the hiring of nearly 1,000 coaches from around 60 contractors. NBC prepared a detailed prospectus, in a standard form, for each company, and these were made available to prospective purchasers.

The Government indicated that there would be separate enabling acts to privatise London Transport, the Scottish Bus Group and PTE fleets. Those local authorities that owned their own bus fleets had to form them into separate legal entities, with transparent accounting, to ensure that there were no hidden subsidies, and they were encouraged to sell their bus operations to management and/or employees, or external purchasers.

Brian has always kept the use of consultants and other expensive advisors to an absolute minimum. Accordingly he went through the accounts of various NBC subsidiaries himself, frequently travelling to England to survey the areas that they served. He looked at first at small companies, like Provincial, and together with Fraser McColl had a very close look at City of Oxford. To this day there remains in a store at the Stagecoach headquarters in Perth a box which contains photographs relating to various NBC companies, including vehicles, bus stations and depots. Most evidently came from bus enthusiasts who were known to Brian, or others who were trying to be helpful.

Stagecoach (Holdings) Ltd, controlled by Brian and Ann, was formed on 4 September 1986. Just under three months later, on 26 November 1986, Skipburn Ltd was formed specifically to bid for NBC subsidiaries, Brian, Ann, Fraser McColl and Dawson Williams, then Managing Director of Hampshire Bus, being the first directors.

Although Brian was the financial brain at Stagecoach, the role played by Ann must not be underestimated. She was not only very hard-working but (as we have seen) also had acquired a reputation with suppliers for being a tenacious negotiator. She told them that she was not interested in perks like dinners and tickets for Wimbledon; all she wanted was the lowest possible price, and she had a very fine instinct for knowing when she had reached it. Ann tells a lovely story about Volvo, which regularly invited customers to various functions (and, indeed, still does). Brian received an invitation to a dinner in Glasgow, whereupon Ann phoned Bernt Brandtzaeg, then Managing Director of Volvo's British truck and bus operations, to advise him that, as joint owner of the company, she would also be attending. Brandtzaeg, an affable Norwegian, tried to advise her that it was an all-male function and that women were not invited, but he had met his match. Ann went to the dinner, and Volvo never again held an all-male dinner!

The Government was so keen to press ahead with the NBC privatisation process that some of the early deals were done at very attractive prices to the purchasers. The first fleet to be privatised, Devon General, was bought on 19 August 1986 by a management team headed by Harry Blundred. Harry had pioneered the use of very frequent services with minibuses, in Exeter and Torbay, and was to feature in the Stagecoach story on a number of occasions.

Skipburn was successful with its bid for Hampshire Bus and Pilgrim Coaches, which together ran 243 vehicles. They were the 29th and 30th NBC subsidiaries to be sold, but only the fourth and fifth fleets not acquired by management teams. Bought on 2 April 1987 for £2.2 million, they were the only companies to be acquired by Skipburn.

Brian and Ann were surprised to find that property developers were interested in a large depot that Hampshire Bus had in a prime site in Southampton. They quickly came to the conclusion that it would be better to sell the freehold property to raise money that could be used to purchase another NBC subsidiary. Would-be developers were invited to submit bids by sealed tender — a most unusual method in England. In Scotland, where the conveyancing system is different (and free from the 'gazumping' that can occur in England and Wales), it is normal to invite bids for the purchase of a property by a fixed time and date; indeed, this was the only system that Ann and Brian understood. Ann took the overnight coach to London and visited several of the top property developers. A good mimic of accents and mannerisms, Ann remembers the incredulity of some of the top London property developers at how they planned to dispose of the Southampton premises, but she stuck to her guns.

About six bidders submitted offers. Brian and Ann sat with lawyers who were handling the sale and started to open the envelopes. The highest bid was for £3.4 million. Ann and Brian leapt to their feet and hugged each other. Both were ecstatic. As Ann recalls, it was like winning the pools. It meant that their houses were no longer required by their bankers as security and that Fraser McColl's bank guarantee was no longer needed. For their part the two lawyers thanked Ann and Brian warmly for allowing them to take part in their special day!

The sale of the Southampton premises came at the height of a property boom, but, despite this, Brian insists that they were not being clever; they simply had no idea that such a windfall was going to happen. There was an outcry over the property sale, but it transpired that most of NBC's properties had not been revalued for many years, and, with very few exceptions, there was no claw-back provision, giving NBC a share of any gain on resale of property, in any of the sale contracts. However, the sale encouraged Ann to develop a skill in the valuation of acquired properties. She also took insurance and pensions under her control.

The relationship with Dawson Williams did not last to the end of 1987. He made a comfortable profit from his investment, but it was exaggerated at the time, *Bus Business* writing that he had become a millionaire. In fact, it was a relatively small sum after tax. He later became a senior executive with Drawlane, another company bidding for NBC subsidiaries.

Shortly after the sale of the Southampton depot Brian Cox joined Stagecoach from SBG. He was appointed Managing Director of Hampshire Bus but continued to live in Scotland for a number of years, being also responsible for the bus operations in Perth and Glasgow. Brian would go on to play a very important role in Stagecoach's road and rail operations.

Ann quickly got into the purchasing side of newly acquired subsidiaries. As already mentioned, her instinct was always to get the best possible deal. At Hampshire Bus she managed to drive down the price of oil by 40%. While she was surprised that NBC had not used its corporate muscle to obtain better deals, she was horrified when a senior executive of SBG took her to one side at an event and warned her sternly that she was spoiling the business for everyone through her aggressive purchasing policies!

In June 1987 Derek Scott — Brian's mentor at Arthur Andersen and one of Stagecoach's auditors from 1982 to 1986 — joined Stagecoach as Finance Director. He had worked with Brian, Ann, Fraser McColl and Dawson Williams on the purchase of Hampshire Bus and arrived in Perth at a very interesting time, when Stagecoach was in the thick of bids for other NBC subsidiaries. Much management time was still being devoted to the express-coach operations, and the bankers had been concerned that the company needed a stronger senior management team, with a Finance Director as the first priority. Derek, who was self-employed, never actually became an employee but provided services to Stagecoach on a fee basis, as recorded annually in the accounts. However, for several years he was very heavily involved in the company's rapid growth. Ann simply describes him as a wonderful person to work with.

On 22 July 1987 Cumberland Motor Services was bought for £2.8 million — the first acquisition made by Stagecoach Holdings Ltd. Stagecoach knew a few weeks earlier that it had been the successful bidder, but completion was delayed because civil servants had to wait for the result of the General Election. Cumberland operated 230 buses on a network of services from Carlisle, through the Lake District, and down to the Furness peninsula. Derek had been born in Carlisle, moving to Scotland when only two years old, but his family had maintained contact with the area, and he thought that he knew it pretty well. He recalls meeting Brian in Carlisle one afternoon at the time when they were looking at bidding for Cumberland. Brian had already been out and about, studying the morning-peak journeys, and had obtained maps from the local tourist office and marked them up with a highlighter pen. After a quick tea Brian and Derek caught a bus out to the suburb of Harraby. The driver's suspicions were probably aroused when he had to tell them that he had reached the terminus. They decided to get off and walk back into the city centre. Observing further buses on the way, Derek was amazed at Brian's analytical skills and the way that he could make a very good assessment of a city and its system in just one day. It was an exercise that was subsequently repeated many times over.

In the three years after the Cumberland acquisition Stagecoach would acquire a number of smaller independent companies in the area, including Yeowarts of Whitehaven and Kirkpatrick of Brigham, near Cockermouth, in May 1988, Stephensons of Maryport in May 1989 and Palmer of Carlisle at the start of 1990. This was unusual. Stagecoach did not normally buy up smaller companies, but felt that amicable consolidation in Cumbria would avoid the costs of what would otherwise be wasteful competition.

Stagecoach has always had a very lean management structure, and that was particularly true back in 1987; there were no teams of people that could be sent in to newly acquired subsidiaries. By contrast, but in common with many nationalised industries, NBC had excessive numbers and layers of management. Many of those people would be made redundant, not just by Stagecoach but also by other purchasers, but people like drivers and mechanics were clearly essential. Under Stagecoach the chain of command went from the head office to the fleet director to the depot manager, and then to drivers and maintenance staff. It remains to this day one of Brian's business philosophies that there should be no more than four links in a chain of command; any more tends to result in poor business decisions and higher administrative costs.

Sometimes senior executives at acquired companies had made unsuccessful rival bids. Some left as soon as Stagecoach came in, while others stayed and their careers prospered. At Cumberland the Managing Director left immediately, but the Chief Engineer, Barry Hinkley, took the reins and soon rose in the rapidly expanding organisation.

Brian feels that Stagecoach's reputation for shedding management jobs was exaggerated. Some very senior managers were of no use to Stagecoach because Brian knew that they could not adapt to the change of climate, but as he and his team dug down into the newly acquired organisations they found some very talented people with good skills and they adapted very well to the new owner's ways of working. Stagecoach brought through their own new leaders, and many of them are still with the Group. Brian also found that there were some excellent secretaries at the top of acquired companies. Whereas the managers had moved around under the NBC system, most of the secretaries had been born and brought up in their areas and had excellent local knowledge and contacts.

A strong bus team now came together. Brian concentrated on finance and networks, with Derek doing due diligence. Barry Hinkley rapidly became a right-hand man, soon assuming responsibility for quality and the cost of engineering and subsequently taking on purchasing for the Group. Brian Cox was running the subsidiaries in the South of England but frequently took on other assignments. More people were about to join this team in what would be a period of rapid growth.

Most of the double-deckers acquired with the United Counties fleet were Bristol VRTs, bodied by Eastern Coach Works to NBC standard. No 950 (VVV 950W), a late model dating from 1981, is seen leaving Northampton bus station for Daventry with a good number of passengers in October 1995.

In October 1987 Stagecoach sold the Southampton-area operations of Hampshire Bus to Southern Vectis, for around £1 million. The Isle of Wight company had been the third fleet to be bought by its management from NBC, on 7 October 1986, and to this day continues to operate the Southampton services, under the Solent Blue Line name. Stagecoach retained what it believed was the more profitable part of Hampshire Bus, and the sale brought in further funds for its war chest.

Back in Scotland some further capacity on the coach side was added when Cotters Coachline was bought from its receivers, along with eight Volvo B10M / Van Hool coaches, the acquisition including a garage at Warroch Street, Glasgow.

On 18 November 1987 United Counties Omnibus Co was bought from NBC, for £4.1 million. The operations that became Luton & District Transport and Milton Keynes City Bus had been hived off into separate companies before the start of the NBC sales, leaving United Counties with 250 buses and a still-substantial network centred on Northampton and covering much of Northamptonshire and Bedfordshire.

NBC's Privatisation Unit was getting better prices for companies sold later in the process. In the case of Cumberland and United Counties it realised that management bids were likely to be too low and alerted Stagecoach to the fact. One member of the management team at United Counties that had bid unsuccessfully for the company was the then Traffic Manager, Ben Colson, but he stayed on under Stagecoach ownership and soon became another valued member of the bus team, advising on several companies that were acquired later.

Stagecoach decided at an early stage to apply its livery to its acquired fleets and thereafter always repainted acquired buses as soon as practicable; this not only helped to establish a corporate identity but also facilitated the transfer of vehicles between subsidiary companies, be it temporarily or on a more permanent basis.

Brian got into the habit of working in Perth on Mondays and Fridays and spending the middle three days of the week with various subsidiaries in England. As he delved into the acquired companies he realised that this was the ideal business for Stagecoach and that he wanted to invest in other bus fleets as and when they became available.

The combination of Brian's business skills and the specialist knowledge of local management set about making the companies more profitable. At first they were set a target of 10% profit on turnover, this later rising to 15% — unheard of at the time. Operations that did not perform were stripped out, these including not merely uneconomic services but also central engineering workshops, seasonal coaching activities and the like.

Brian got the local managers in acquired companies to drive him round their networks. In some

In the company's infancy the Stagecoach stripes even appeared on a staff car!

cases restrictive practices had been introduced with one-man operation, resulting in unacceptably long running times, so more Routemasters, readily available from London at low prices, were bought and introduced into acquired companies. The Routemasters broke the back of restrictive practices; many hours were taken out of duties, but the service level to passengers was enhanced because crew-operated journey times were considerably quicker.

The British bus manufacturing industry suffered great pain from the deregulation of most bus services and the privatisation of most of the operating industry, and in the 1980s demand for large buses fell to such low levels — largely as a result of investment decisions' being postponed in the run-up to privatisation and in the years afterwards — that several long-established manufacturers went out of business. Orders were concentrated on minibuses that could penetrate more deeply into residential areas and provide more frequent services. They worked like shared taxis, but they were also very good for attacking the area of a resident operator running a fleet of large buses; the small vehicles could cream off enough business to cover their operating costs, at the same time reducing the revenue taken by full size buses and making their services unprofitable. Furthermore, management teams who had the opportunity to bid for their businesses (or rather their financiers) did not want their cash flows committed to large numbers of new buses before buy-out debts were repaid. They were helped in this by the fact that, throughout the 1970s, all new buses and dual-purpose coaches had been eligible for Bus Grant; this had effectively reduced the average age of many fleets, so that new owners could delay buying new buses, either to give priority to repaying their bankers, or to accumulate funds to buy other bus fleets.

Many of the buses in the fleets bought from NBC were Bristol VRTs and Leyland Nationals. Both types were expensive to operate, in terms of engineering costs, compared with other vehicles familiar to Stagecoach in their Scottish operations. That led to a number of innovations, like the introduction of Routemasters and, more surprisingly, the acquisition (from South Yorkshire PTE) of some front-engined Volvo

double-deckers which were drafted in to Hampshire Bus, albeit as a relatively short-term measure.

Stagecoach, with its extensive experience of long-distance express services, knew the importance of having new vehicles to attract and retain customers. The most popular double-deck chassis at that time was the Leyland Olympian, so early in 1988 an order was placed for 30 long-wheelbase models (with up to 87 seats) bodied by Alexander at Falkirk and starting a long association with that builder. Leyland and Alexander had already collaborated on the production of 12m tri-axle Olympian double-deckers for Hong Kong. Stagecoach saw their potential to avoid duplication at peak periods and so ordered two with 96 seats, later delivered to Cumberland, and one with 110 seats — the highest-capacity bus in the country — that joined the Magicbus fleet in Glasgow. Within months a repeat order was placed with Leyland and Alexander for a further 40 two-axle Olympians, this combination remaining the Stagecoach standard double-decker for several years. The first order with Leyland was placed with the management team that had bought out the company from state ownership,

The acquisition of former NBC companies brought substantial numbers of Bristol VRTs with Eastern Coach Works bodywork, normally built to a height of around 13ft 8in. Betrayed by its registration number as a bus that started life with Devon General, Hampshire Bus 448 (LFJ 870W) is seen here in Basingstoke in August 1995. Although Brian was critical of the type's high maintenance costs, a handful survived in the Stagecoach Group until 2005.

The standard NBC single-deck bus in the 1970s was the Leyland National. Although structurally very sound, and superbly protected against corrosion, their weak spot was the horizontal 510 engine. Hampshire Bus 164 (VFX 984S) looked smart when photographed in Southampton in February 1996.

but in March 1988 they resold the business to Volvo Bus Corporation, which retained the Leyland name until a higher Volvo content was introduced in the Olympian chassis, in preparation for the introduction of Euro 1 emissions limits in October 1993.

The acquisition of Hampshire Bus, Cumberland, and United Counties had taken Stagecoach to the maximum number of companies that it could buy direct from NBC. Although it was time for consolidation, the team at Perth was always looking for opportunities, and not just in the UK. In 1988 Stagecoach took a 50% shareholding in Speedybus Enterprises of Hong Kong, whose principal activity was the sale of advertising space on former Hong Kong double-deckers that were being exported to run in several cities on the Chinese mainland. It was an unusual venture, but it gave Stagecoach first-hand experience in China at a time when that country was much less open than it is today. Brian, typically, saw it as a stepping-stone.

Ann's dealings in property sometimes brought Stagecoach into conflict with the authorities, and one well-documented instance came in the summer of 1988. The acquisition of Cumberland Motor Services had included a bus station in the centre of Keswick, used not just by Cumberland's own services but also by many coaches visiting this popular tourist centre. A useful facility for coach operators, it nevertheless

made no money for Cumberland or Stagecoach. Stagecoach therefore teamed up with Conder Developments to build a shopping and health centre, while still retaining space to operate bus services, but the local authority had its own preferred developer and turned down the Stagecoach application, even though Stagecoach owned the land. Ann's reaction to this decision was to arrange for around 20 old buses to be driven or towed from the reserve fleet at Spittalfield to Keswick, effectively blockading the bus station in the middle of the summer tourist season. There was uproar, particularly from local traders — some of them local councillors — about loss of business, but once again Stagecoach stuck to its guns. The planners eventually backed down, and the Stagecoach/Conder redevelopment was approved.

Ann is remarkably frank about the whole saga. Visiting Keswick with Barry Hinkley to see if the blockade was effective, she jumped off an old Routemaster and, being a trained nurse, instinctively knew that she had broken her ankle. Barry's first reaction was to take her to the hospital in Keswick, but she was totally against giving the local media a publicity coup, so, despite the pain, she arranged for a driver to take her all the way home to Perth to have the joint reset. She is a tough lady, but she also has a soft side, as we shall see later. Nevertheless, Keswick put her name very clearly in the minds of other planners around the country; they all knew about her and were unwilling to cross her!

While Keswick and other strong-arm tactics were not illegal, they were widely reported in the media and came to the attention of a small number of Labour politicians who never missed an opportunity to snipe at the company. This was ironic, because most of the passengers who benefited from the Stagecoach express services were likely to be Labour voters. However, Ann and Brian had by now become high-profile figures, with substantial wealth tied up in the expanding company, and, while some of their actions were brash, much of the political outcry was probably the result of envy, especially in Scotland.

In the summer of 1988 Harry Blundred of Devon General announced plans to set up a network of services, operated by minibuses, in Basingstoke, part of the territory of Hampshire Bus. He had also started to compete with City of Oxford, so Stagecoach and the Oxford company retaliated by setting up a competitive service in Devon.

In order to get round the requirement of giving the Traffic Commissioner 42 days' notice to start a new service, a *free* service (using eight Leyland Nationals hastily repainted all-over white) was introduced along Torquay's promenade to Paignton in the peak summer season. This had a devastating effect on the profitability of Devon General, which normally made a lot of money in Torquay in the summer months and nothing like so much for the rest of the year. Fares were high in Devon. Older people were price-sensitive but not time-sensitive and therefore waited for the free buses.

Harry Blundred responded by going to court, successfully alleging that City of Oxford and Hampshire Bus had entered into a conspiracy to damage his business. The two partners had to pull out, but Stagecoach then advised Harry Blundred that it would launch a rival minibus operation in Basingstoke. Both would almost certainly have lost money, so they came to a stand-off whereby the Devon company abandoned its plans to run in Hampshire.

In August 1988 Stagecoach International was formed, to seek further business opportunities outside the UK. It was headed by Peter Lutman, an experienced former NBC executive.

As already mentioned, Brian has always had the ability to plan strategically and the vision to predict opportunities for Stagecoach. He recognised that the company would need to increase its share capital and bank borrowing facilities to expand further. He and Ann were introduced to Ewan Brown, a director of Noble Grossart, a merchant bank in Edinburgh, and set out their plans. It might have helped that he was also a native of Perth, but Brian and Ann made a tremendous impression on him. At their very first meeting, Brian explained how he saw the consolidation of the industry, with control of the bus fleets ending up in the hands of a few large groups. Brian knew there would be opportunities to buy more of the former NBC companies. He predicted significant economies of scale, the benefits of buying new buses, and the gains to be made from breaking restrictive practices. In that very first meeting, he used the word 'oligopoly'.

Ewan Brown had some time previously been a non-executive director of the Scottish Transport Group,

the parent of SBG, but had left the STG Board when privatisation was first proposed. That was perceptive, because he could have been involved in a conflict of interest with any potential purchaser. He recalls the formality of the STG meetings, and the regular predictions at their Carron House headquarters of impending doom for Stagecoach.

Noble Grossart came up with a deal that was totally different from the way that venture capitalists invest in a company. It raised £5 million in convertible preference shares, structured in a way that encouraged Brian and Ann to get the value of Stagecoach as high as possible before flotation. Ewan Brown brought together a group of seven

Above: In 1988, Stagecoach made its first investment in new double-deck service buses, including United Counties 623 (F623 MSL), seen in Northampton in October 1989. The long-wheelbase Leyland Olympian chassis at that time had a Gardner engine and Alexander bodywork seating 87 passengers.

Upper left: Three tri-axle Leyland Olympians were delivered to Stagecoach in 1989. F110 NES had the highest capacity of any bus in Britain, with 66 seats on the upper deck and 44 downstairs. It is seen in June 1990, working with Magicbus in Glasgow. Despite its 12m length, the bus was remarkably manœuvrable, because the second axle, ahead of the drive axle, steered at lower speeds, helping the vehicle to negotiate tight turns.

Lower left: The 110-seat tri-axle Leyland Olympian undergoing its tilt test inside the Alexander factory. Every seat on the upper deck was loaded with test weights, following which the bus had to tilt to 28° without tipping over.

A Daimler CVG6 double-decker, newly arrived from Kowloon Motor Bus and freshly repainted into Stagecoach colours for service in Malawi. Local people had never previously seen double-deck buses and were initially very cautious about riding on the upper deck. However, they soon proved popular and capable of moving large numbers of passengers.

Scottish institutions that invested a total of £5 million in Stagecoach, doubling the company's capital.

The Group's then bankers, at Standard Chartered Bank, were fully supportive, committing to give Stage-coach a £50 million facility to fund acquisitions. However, as things turned out this was ultimately provided by the Bank of Scotland rather than by Standard Chartered, which had wanted to syndicate the facility to involve other banks, whereas Stage-coach preferred to deal with one principal banker.

Conventional banking practice was to rely on assets as security for a loan, but the Bank of Scotland recognised the regular flow of cash coming in to Stagecoach. It was also comfortable because Stagecoach had established a good track record, repaying some earlier loans more quickly than required, thanks to windfalls like the property deals in Southampton and Keswick.

Ann and Brian had their feet firmly on the ground. Both Derek and Ewan Brown recall a meeting to woo potential investors in the Caledonian Hotel at the west end of Princes Street, Edinburgh. Told that Ann would have to leave at a certain time to go to London, the institutional investors present doubtless expected a taxi to take her to the airport for one of the last flights. Imagine their surprise when an overnight coach to London took a slight detour to collect her from the front of the hotel!

Ewan Brown accepted an invitation to become the first non-executive director of Stagecoach, a position he retains to this day. He also became Brian's closest external confidant, whom Brian would use regularly as a sounding-board for new ideas and projects, and effectively took over from Fraser McColl as Brian's mentor.

Brian, Ann and Ewan Brown are very comfortable with each other. Brian says that Ewan puts a lot of polish into the business. In his own right a very innovative thinker, he also added finesse to Brian's proposals and presented them to investors. Their communication was (and still is) usually by telephone — sometimes with calls as brief as a minute — whereby Brian would explain ideas and plans. Ewan recalls that the vision and drive came largely from Brian but that Brian involved people, especially Ann, Derek and himself, in every decision. All might have a slightly different view, but consensus would be reached. Ewan could provide a more external perspective, but he also greatly admired the very strong management flair of Ann and Derek. He saw himself not in the role of a banker but as an adviser. He also credits Brian with never having sprung a surprise on his co-directors or bankers. Everyone was fully involved and informed.

While all the negotiations were handled by Brian, Ann and Derek, the Edinburgh firm ensured that

A line of Daimler double-deckers and drivers awaiting their next turn of duty at the UTM depot in Blantyre, Malawi.

deals were processed properly, obtaining share-holder support and, later, maintaining contact with the Stock Exchange.

Brian had drawn up alternative business strategies. His most ambitious was to run all the buses in Scotland, but that was never likely to be possible, because of the way that NBC had been broken up before privatisation; SBG was likely to be similarly fragmented. His alternative plan was acquisition of some NBC and SBG subsidiaries, but thereafter expansion would have to come globally. The most attractive opportunities were likely to be in the Commonwealth countries, because they spoke English, had British accounting and legal systems and drove on the left.

The British Electric Traction group had sold its British bus interests to the Government in 1968, leading to the formation in 1969 of the National Bus Company, but it had retained United Transport, running trucks and buses in several African countries. In March 1989 Stagecoach bought BET's 51% of United Transport Malawi, with the Government of Malawi retaining the balance. Stagecoach thereby acquired a controlling interest in more than 300 buses for around £800,000.

The contrast in ownership could hardly have been greater. BET directors enjoyed a luxurious lifestyle, including big-game hunting and other safaris, but were rumoured rarely, if ever, to have been inside their bus depots. Their main concern, in the negotiations with Stagecoach, was that they would not damage the reputation of BET.

Brian soon took the view that UTM had been under-performing. There was a mixture of city services in Blantyre and Lilongwe, rural services, and inter-city express routes. Stagecoach brought over from Hong Kong, in several batches, 60 old but well-maintained Daimler double-deckers, to increase capacity on the city services, and restructured the rural routes so that fewer buses ran in the rainy season, when roads were often impassable and there was less demand for travel. Once Brian had drawn up the turnaround plans for UTM he stopped going to Malawi because his time was urgently needed to work on the next stage of growth in the UK. Ann went out to Malawi once a month, to put the turnaround plans into effect.

The next two acquisitions were at home, and they really made the bus industry sit up and take notice of Stagecoach. Under the rules for selling off NBC no one purchaser was permitted to acquire more than three subsidiaries first-hand, but there was nothing to prevent the acquisition of further NBC companies second-hand from their management teams or other owners. Brian, of course, had foreseen this oppor-tunity for growth in his strategic planning.

In April 1989 Stagecoach bought East Midland Motor Services from its management team for an estimated £6 million. The acquisition included 260 buses operating in northeast Derbyshire and north and central Nottinghamshire. The business had been purchased from NBC on 5 February 1988 by then Managing Director Peter Jenner and some colleagues, who subsequently acquired Rainworth Travel, within its territory, as well as establishing two subsidiaries that were well outside its area; Frontrunner (South East) was based in Essex, from where it provided tendered services on behalf of London Transport, while Frontrunner (North West) operated in Glossop, Derbyshire. Jenner had been

keen to sell out before the end of the 1988/9 tax year; Derek recalls that the whole deal was done within seven days! Stagecoach soon sold the Essex operations to Ensign Bus and those based on Glossop to Drawlane, another of the emerging groups that was buying up former NBC subsidiaries.

East Midland ran services in the constituencies of two well-known left-wing Labour politicians, Tony Benn and Dennis Skinner. They asked for a meeting in the House of Commons with the new owners, to which local trade-union officials were also invited. Brian, ever the casual dresser, turned up in a donkey jacket, and the MPs, assuming that he was a trade-union representative, chatted freely to him. By the time someone asked who he was Brian had the situation completely under control!

Just two weeks after the East Midland acquisition Ribble Motor Services, one of the most famous bus companies in England, joined Stagecoach when it was bought for £7.2 million from its management team. The latter had bought the company, including 700 buses, from NBC on 2 March 1988 and had subsequently bought competitive minibus oper-ations in Preston and Manchester from United Bus, a subsidiary of British Electric Traction that had been hastily created to try to take advantage of deregulation. Ribble had also sold its coaching operations, almost immediately after purchase from NBC, to Amberline of Liverpool, and its central parts operation to Gilbraith, a major Leyland dealer in nearby Chorley. At one time Ribble's territory had stretched all the way from Liverpool and Manchester to the Scottish border, but depots in Carlisle, Penrith and Keswick had been hived off and added to Cumberland Motor Services before privatisation. Brian was staggered by the number of forms circulating within Ribble and the culture of form-filling; he cured that by shutting down the printing department, making five people redundant!

East Midland was another subsidiary that ran a limited number of Routemasters. No 980 (WLT 980) is seen in Mansfield in September 1990.

Above: The former Stagecoach headquarters at Charlotte House, in Charlotte Street, Perth. The ground floor was principally a shop for local bus passengers, with offices on the three levels above.

Right: A delightful cameo photograph of Ann and Brian, taken with a Polaroid camera in the large office that they shared in Charlotte House, Perth.

Above: This Neoplan Jetliner is seen in Dunfermline bus station in June 1990, after the express services had been acquired by National Express; this was during the one-year period when Stagecoach names were still carried by the Caledonian Express fleet. Just over a year later the Fife Scottish buses in the background became part of the rapidly expanding Stagecoach empire.

A few weeks later a further acquisition was made in the North West of England when the depot and 24 buses of Barrow Borough Transport were acquired from its receivers for around £1.2 million. East Midland added 300 vehicles (including the short-lived Frontrunner operations) and Ribble more than 800. That, plus the fleet in Malawi, meant that Stagecoach more than doubled the number of vehicles that it owned in the space of just six weeks.

Stagecoach Express continued to take up a wholly disproportionate amount of Brian's time, but the market was changing. British Rail had introduced new and much more efficient 'Sprinter' trains that were giving stiff competition on the Glasgow–Perth–Dundee–Aberdeen route, and it was also obvious that National Express was going to come into Scotland. With this in prospect Stagecoach's express operations within Scotland and into England were sold in August 1989 to National Express, along with the depot at Walnut Grove, Perth, and 31 coaches. National Express was given a period of one year in which to wean customers from the Stagecoach name to the National Express and new Caledonian Express brands.

There was a lot of sadness when National Express took over the coach operations. Some people who had been with Stagecoach from early times stayed with the new owners, while others continued to work for Stagecoach on local services and contracts. Brian has said that selling was a difficult decision, but the directors recognised that Stagecoach had become a stage-carriage operator and had to concentrate on that business. He was proud of the fact that for nearly nine years, except for just one night, the company had always been able to operate its Scotland–London services. There were times when the A74 and M6 had been blocked by snow, but the coaches had used alternative routes, including travelling by Kilmarnock and Dumfries and, at times, using the A1 from Edinburgh down the east coast.

When Walnut Grove was sold the corporate headquarters moved to an elegant four-storey building, Charlotte House, in Charlotte Street, Perth, overlooking a large stretch of parkland known as the North Inch. It was also a little too close to the River Tay, which on one or two occasions was to burst its banks, flooding Charlotte Street and the basement and ground floor.

Charlotte House was a most unlikely building to be the headquarters of a rapidly expanding bus business. The ground floor served as a local bus travel shop, reception area and telephone exchange. Brian and Ann still shared a desk, as they had at Walnut Grove, but this time sat in a large green-painted room, with a high ceiling, facing northwards. There was a lively buzz about the place, with its warren of rooms and staircases.

It was known that the Scottish Bus Group was going to be sold out of state ownership, but that was not happening quickly enough for Brian and Ann. Following the sale of the express-coach business both were keen to have a presence in their home city, so some surplus Leyland Nationals were driven north to set up competitive services against Strathtay Scottish. Although in full Stagecoach colours they were branded as Perth Panthers to avoid any problems with the short-term use of the Stagecoach name by National Express.

There was a keen battle for several months, but by this time Stagecoach had sufficiently deep pockets to be able to take on this kind of fight. Neil Renilson, Managing Director of Strathtay Scottish, must have seen the way that the wind was blowing, because he resigned from SBG in March 1989.

Neil is one of the most forthright characters in the industry and is currently Managing Director of Lothian Buses, centred on Edinburgh. Having originally learned the business with Lothian, he then worked his way up through various NBC subsidiaries on the traffic side before joining Strathtay. When he handed in his resignation to SBG he was sternly warned that he could never again work for the group. Were its employees the last to know that it was being privatised?

Neil was supposed to spend six months out of the industry before joining any competitor, but he was involved almost immediately in many of Stagecoach's plans. In September 1989 he officially took responsibility for all the Scottish operations.

Top: The Perth Panther network was established to compete in Stagecoach's home city with Strathtay Scottish. Photographed in June 1990 in full corporate livery, 219 (VKE 568S) did not carry any Stagecoach names because at this time National Express had just taken over Stagecoach's express network and still had the right to use the Stagecoach name.

Above: The acquisition of the Ribble fleet in the spring of 1989 brought a substantial number of Leyland Atlanteans with NBC-standard bodywork by Park Royal. No 1378 (NRN 378P), still in red and grey, was working in Preston in June 1990.

The Southdown fleet that was acquired by Stagecoach included 12 Volvo Citybus B10M-50 double-deck buses with Northern Counties bodywork, dating from 1989. They were built to a dual-purpose specification with high-backed seats for longer journeys, clearly seen in this view. This smartly presented bus is seen with a good number of passengers at Eastbourne in August 1995.

In August 1989 yet another famous former NBC subsidiary was added to the Stagecoach stable when Southdown Motor Services was bought for £6.326 million from a management team led by Philip Ayers. They had acquired it on 2 October 1987 from NBC. Southdown also held 51% in Top Line, a low-cost bus operation in Hastings, the balance of the shares being held by Eastbourne Borough. Stagecoach bought out the municipal shareholding and also acquired a small independent, Cedar of Worthing. Together these acquisitions increased the Group fleet by around 250 vehicles. Brian Cox added Southdown to his portfolio and, at the same time, handed on the baton in Scotland to Neil Renilson, enabling Brian Cox to move and live near Chichester.

Southdown had its headquarters at Lewes and

served a territory stretching from Portsmouth to Eastbourne. It also had a network of express services to and from London, but it was not in good shape, and other companies ran the bulk of services in busy urban centres like Brighton and Portsmouth. No doubt the plan was to consolidate on the South Coast, but that soon ran into problems.

The Stagecoach bus team had become highly skilled at moving into acquired companies and working out what they wanted to retain and what was surplus to their requirements. Although some properties — part of Ann's portfolio — were retained, several traditional engineering centres were closed down. Stagecoach saw little point in keeping facilities that not only duplicated each other, like re-manufacturing engines, but were also less competitive than external specialists.

This was the first of two Bristol VRT double-deck buses in the Southdown fleet with convertible-open-top bodywork. The guard-rails and glazing could be removed and replaced with fixed tops for winter working.
No 7621 (UWV 621S) is seen in Eastbourne on a warm summer's day in August 1995.

In October 1989 Stagecoach bought Portsmouth Citybus for £663,000. The company had been sold by Portsmouth City Council the previous year, Southampton City Transport taking 75% and the workforce 25%, but it had continued to lose money.

Because Southdown ran services into Portsmouth from the east and had a depot on the edge of the city, the Monopolies & Mergers Commission ruled that Stagecoach must give undertakings that, should a competitor come onto any route and Stagecoach lower its fares in response, the company would have to retain those lower fares, even after the competitor pulled out. However, Nicholas Ridley, then Secretary of State for Trade & Industry, overruled the MMC and ordered Stagecoach to divest itself of Portsmouth Citybus. It is difficult to understand how he reached his decision, because the local authorities, unions and bus users in the area had all been in favour of Stagecoach. Brian puts it down to a 'Stagecoach fear factor'. If Portsmouth Citybus had not been bought it would have folded. Ridley was probably taking revenge for the failure of his dream, when Transport Minister earlier in the Thatcher Government, of thousands of managers each owning their own buses. It was to be his last decision on the industry before being forced to resign for making offensive remarks about Germany.

Portsmouth Citybus and 104 buses were eventually sold to Harry Blundred's Transit Holdings in December 1990. Brian recalled that Harry Blundred was looking for growth, noting that Nicholas Ridley's ruling had cost Stagecoach just over £1 million.

Further evidence of Conservative hostility to Stagecoach came in 1989 when West Midlands PTE came up for sale. Accountants KPMG had valued the business at £60 million, but Brian felt the company was worth £85 million and was prepared to pay that. He appealed to the OFT and the West Midlands district auditor, saying that the PTA, the owner of the PTE, was legally obliged to accept the best offer. Malcolm Rifkind had become Minister of Transport, and his deputy, Michael Portillo, rejected Stagecoach's appeal, saying that it was for the PTA to decide which offer to accept. The district auditor must have been sympathetic to the Stagecoach position, because a management/employee buy-out eventually had to pay £70.7 million — still nearly £15 million less than Stagecoach had been prepared to pay!

There was a limited amount of competition on local services in Scotland, but a company called Inverness Traction had started running services in the town in competition with Highland Scottish, the SBG subsidiary. It used a fleet of minibuses but collapsed under the weight of competition from Highland Scottish. Its vehicles and services were taken over by another new operator, cheekily using the name Alexander (North East) to compete with SBG's Northern Scottish subsidiary. Later Alexander (North East) also failed, taking Inverness Traction with it.

Stagecoach saw the opportunity to become established in Inverness and in November 1989 paid the receivers a nominal amount for the assets of Inverness Traction. In some respects it is surprising that this saga did not become the subject of yet another OFT enquiry. The action by Highland Scottish against Inverness Traction was found to be predatory by the MMC, but the entry of Stagecoach created competition and so provided a market solution that allowed the regulators to recommend no action and return to London.

In December 1989 another former NBC subsidiary, Hastings & District, was bought from its management team, for £1.165 million. Richard Bailey and some colleagues had bought the company from NBC on 16 December 1987. Much of the fleet consisted of a large number of Mercedes-Benz minibuses that were quite new, but the new owners had run into problems on repaying the leases.

Hastings & District lay at the eastern end of Southdown's territory. The MMC allowed Stagecoach to retain Hastings & District, following a decision in the House of Lords in a case brought by South Yorkshire PTE requesting a definition of what constituted a substantial part of the UK bus market. However, the MMC again asked for undertakings from Stagecoach that, if a competitor started on any route in Hastings, and if Stagecoach lowered its fares, it would retain those lower fares even after the competitor pulled out. The MMC and other authorities probably realised that the business could have collapsed and the people of Hastings been left without a bus service if Stagecoach had not come in.

By this time Ann was frequently used as the public face of the company, being female and older than Brian. She was just as gutsy when strong action was required, as she had shown in Keswick, but her image was boosted when she was nominated the Veuve Clicquot Business Woman of the Year in 1990. It was very unusual to have a woman in such a senior position in a transport company, and the media loved it. Ann's image was also enhanced by being heavily involved in charitable work in Malawi. Medical equipment and old spectacles were collected in Scotland and shipped out whenever any vehicle was transferred to the Malawi fleet, and Stagecoach directors and staff visiting UTM often exceeded their luggage allowances.

In 1985 Stagecoach's express-coach business and local services around Perth had been turning over around £3.5 million per annum. Five years later the company had grown almost thirtyfold, with annual turnover to the end of April 1990 forecast to be close to £100 million. Stagecoach was really rolling!

Ann Gloag visited Malawi regularly when Stagecoach owned UTM and has since maintained her contacts with the country in her charitable works. The Bristol Lodekka in the background had made the long overland journey from the South African port of Durban northward to Blantyre, loaded with medical supplies from Blantyre, the Scottish birthplace of David Livingstone, who discovered Malawi, and from many other parts of Scotland.

Floating on the London Stock Exchange

THERE was relatively little activity on the acquisition front in 1990. Early in the year Stagecoach closed the depot acquired from Cotters at Warroch Street, Glasgow, and moved to a new garage, with much more space, in Hobden Street, Springburn, two miles north of the city centre.

Not all property deals hit the headlines. United Counties had extensive offices, workshops and a depot on a prime site in Bedford Road, Northampton. That was sold for redevelopment in June 1990, and a much smaller and simpler depot established in Rothersthorpe Avenue.

Right from the earliest days Stagecoach had motivated employees with bonuses, and, as the company grew, these arrangements became more sophisticated. In 1991 employees were offered shares in the company before flotation on a 'buy one, get one free' basis. Ann went round all the depots promoting the scheme, and there was a large take-up. The employee price was 7p per share, and the company floated at 22.4p per share, peaking at just under 300p. The share price became a great motivator, but, equally, in the tumble between 1999 and 2003, until the recent recovery, it worked the other way.

Peace was reached with Strathtay Scottish in Perth, with the two companies co-existing on the local network. Stagecoach Scotland Ltd was formed in March 1991. Because National Express had access to the Stagecoach name for express services in Scotland, it was not until this time that services in the Perth area were branded 'Stagecoach'.

The United Kingdom, like much of Western Europe,

Brian and Derek Scott (left) toured many financial institutions in the run-up to flotation. The media was captivated by the Stagecoach story and there were frequent photo-calls, often with a new bus as a backdrop.

started to enter into a deep recession in 1990. Interest rates also went up quite sharply. Fortunately bus services are relatively recession-proof, because people still need to travel. Looking back at the forecasts, Derek says they got the profits just about right but their sources quite wrong; much less revenue came from property sales, but all the bus companies performed better than predicted.

Because Stagecoach was known as an acquisitive company, prospective sellers frequently got in contact. The Toronto Transit Commission wanted to sell a subsidiary, Gray Coach Lines, that ran a network of express services in eastern Canada and into the northeastern United States. It also operated a regular service between the city centre and Pearson International Airport. It was surprising that Stagecoach decided to get back into a coach operation, having sold Stagecoach Express just over a year before, but the Canadian routes had exclusive licences, and the market was regulated.

After some delay the Transport (Scotland) Act 1989 was passed, and 10 subsidiaries of Scottish Bus Group were prepared for privatisation. Purchasers were prevented from buying more than two subsidiaries and could not buy fleets with neighbouring territories. A detailed prospectus was made available for each subsidiary. As in England, management teams were encouraged to bid for their companies and were offered a discount of 5%. The sale included some smaller companies, such as Lowland and Highland, which were not of interest to external buyers like Stagecoach. The Group considered a bid for Strathtay Scottish but was advised against proceeding when it sought informal advice from the OFT. There were some attractive operations, but, with acquisitions limited to two, bids had to be made selectively.

In March 1991 Bluebird Northern was bought, for £5.667 million. This company had once been part of the large network of W. Alexander & Sons, and its

A Bristol Lodekka from the Perth fleet was converted with a door on the offside, but retained its original staircase. It is seen after arriving in Canada and becoming a member of the Gray Coach Lines fleet where it was used for sightseeing and promotional work.

Acquired with the Bluebird Northern fleet in 1991, this Leyland Olympian with Eastern Coach Works bodywork, new in 1982, was carrying a cherished Stagecoach numberplate when seen in Perth in February 1997. The triangular route-number/destination display identify this bus as having originated with an SBG fleet.

coaches carried that firm's traditional Bluebird motif on the main side panels. Although the operations in the North East of Scotland had for many years been legally described as Alexander (Northern) and then Northern Scottish, local people still referred to 'Bluebird', and there was strong loyalty to the brand. Bluebird operated a network of services based on Aberdeen and covering the North East of Scotland as far west as Inverness. Neil Renilson became Managing Director of Bluebird. Brian sat with him and wrote an eight-point business plan to increase the company's profit from around £500,000 per annum; this was done on the back of an envelope, and Neil was instructed not to lose it!

Highland Scottish was privatised in August 1991, being bought by Sandy Rapson and Clansman Travel. They planned to make one third of the workforce redundant and reduce the pay of those who were retained. The Scottish organisers of the Transport & General Workers' Union telephoned Brian to tell him what was happening. Brian immediately saw the opportunity to consolidate in the Inverness area; he said that Stagecoach would employ the drivers, and 50 were recruited immediately. Some new buses awaiting delivery from Alexander in Falkirk, plus spare vehicles, were driven overnight to Inverness and entered service that morning. They initially ran free, but two to three days later the Traffic Commissioner accepted emergency registrations. Over the next few days Highland Scottish withdrew completely from Inverness and Easter Ross. The new fleet was merged with Inverness Traction and placed under the control of Bluebird Northern.

One of the most attractive SBG subsidiaries was Fife Scottish, running a network of services throughout the 'kingdom' and also over the Forth and Tay bridges to Edinburgh and Dundee respectively. Stagecoach entered into what would be a protracted battle, being named preferred bidder for Fife Scottish in May 1991. Some local Labour politicians were keen to support a rival bid by the management and employees, even though it was lower than that of Stagecoach.

Bluebird 171 (866 NHT) was still wearing the old style of Stagecoach fleetname when photographed in Dundee in February 1997. A Leyland Leopard PSU3F/4R with Duple Dominant II Express bodywork new to Alexander (Northern), it dated from 1981, when its wider, twin-leaf entrance door would have qualified it for Bus Grant.

Eventually, in July 1991, Stagecoach secured the Fife business, for £9.111 million, adding 300 buses to the Group total.

Vehicle replacement now became a priority. Most NBC and SBG subsidiaries had depots full of large single-deck buses and double-deckers. In the days of state ownership those routes with heavy traffic had frequently subsidised those that did not earn sufficient revenue, but that had started to change dramatically with the advent of deregulation. Between 1984 and 1990 more than 10,000 minibuses entered service in the UK, and in many cases these ran at increased frequencies, replacing full-size buses. The original minibuses were conversions of popular panel vans, seating around 16-20 passengers, and some models lacked the durability to stand up to the stop-start pressures of all-day bus operation.

The acquisition of Fife Scottish brought more SBG standard Leyland Leopards with Alexander AYS bodywork. No 159 (CSF 159W) dated from 1981 and is seen in Kirkcaldy in May 1996. Although for many years SBG had been practically alone in specifying Leyland's four-speed manual gearbox on Leopards, later orders, including this one, called for the popular Pneumocyclic semi-automatic 'box.

Later vehicles were larger and stronger, with wider, coachbuilt bodywork on van-derived chassis.

The deregulated industry started to match the size of the bus to the number of passengers on each route. That led to the development, initially by Dennis, of the midibus. The Dart was a purpose-built chassis with a relatively low floor and a rear-mounted engine. The first models were built to an overall length of 8.5m, but the design was fairly soon stretched to nearly 10m (and subsequently even further). Volvo soon offered a rival midibus chassis, the B6, using a large number of parts from the FL6 truck but again with a rear-mounted engine. This was still at the pre-production stage in September 1991, when Stagecoach ordered 200 B6s and 55 Dennis Darts, with an option for a further 100, all with 9.8m-long Alexander bodies. One month later the order for new vehicles was increased

by a further 46 Dennis Darts and 70 Leyland Olympian double-deckers, 50 to be bodied by Alexander and 20 by Northern Counties.

Another manufacturer to receive an order from Stagecoach for the first time was ERF, a well-established truck builder that had developed a range of rugged high-frame bus chassis for African conditions. Stagecoach ordered 70, bodied in Malawi for UTM by PEW, in which UTM had a minority shareholding.

In November 1991 Stagecoach bought two more African subsidiaries from British Electric Traction. For just £300,000 the Group acquired 75% of Kenya Bus Services (Nairobi) and 51% of Kenya Bus Services (Mombasa), the respective City Councils holding the balance of the shares. These acquisitions brought a further 400 vehicles into the Group.

In both Malawi and Kenya Stagecoach found

Volvo introduced the Ailsa B55 double-deck bus with a 6.7-litre engine, mounted at the front, alongside the driver. The Scottish Bus Group bought several batches, all with Alexander bodywork. Fife 863 (OSC 63V) was new in 1979 and is seen in Kirkcaldy in May 1996. Note the unusual three-piece entrance door, unique to this model.

Above: The 9.8m-long Dennis Dart with Alexander Dash bodywork quickly became popular with Stagecoach. One of the first batch, dating from 1991/2, is seen leaving Winchester bus station in February 1998, working for Hampshire Bus.

Left: In 1993 East Midland took 18 Volvo B6 midibuses with Alexander Dash bodywork seating 40. This example is seen in Mansfield in October 1999. By 2004 these buses were being sold by Stagecoach for further use elsewhere.

Scottish accountants who were familiar with local ways, and that gave it a little more comfort. Managers from the UK were sometimes seconded to Malawi and Kenya to help local management, and this also greatly broadened their experience.

Ann spent one week in four in Malawi and Kenya. As the third-largest employer in Malawi Stagecoach had considerable influence with the Government. Applications to raise fares had to be approved by the Government, but Ann soon found that the Official State Hostess was one of the power-brokers and was able to arrange for the necessary approval.

In Malawi drivers and mechanics were so hungry that many of them were weak and could not do a full day's work. Stagecoach established a canteen, serving basic food like maize, and productivity improved dramatically. When older buses were shipped out from the UK they were filled with blankets and other medical equipment. Stagecoach also funded the construction and running of a burns unit in Blantyre's Queen Elizabeth Hospital — the company's way of putting something back into the local

community. One day Ann came across a driver who was cradling a new-born baby, abandoned on one of the buses. She took it to an orphanage, run by a little old nun, and was horrified to find that they had no food. The next day she arranged for two pick-up trucks to take food to the orphanage, which is still run to this day by one of her charitable foundations.

In Nairobi the Indian community used to sell lots of parts to the bus companies. One of them spotted Ann's weakness for jewellery and offered to bring her gold from India. Furious at the suggestion that she should cheat on her brother and her company, she had him marched off the premises!

Corruption was rife in Africa, but Stagecoach never paid a penny. Kenya Bus Services had a massive depot in Nairobi, with one expatriate and 3,500 staff. On one of her early visits Ann was told that many of the buses would soon be off the road unless bribes were paid to port officials in Mombasa to get spare parts released. She refused point blank and asked for an appointment to see the President, Daniel arap Moi. She warned him that, in three days, most of the buses

Right: Probably the most mysterious photograph in the collection at Stagecoach headquarters at Perth was this Leyland Fleetline, freshly painted into the colours of Kenya Bus. The vehicles in the background suggest that it might well have been photographed on the premises of Kowloon Motor Bus in Hong Kong, a company that had already supplied substantial numbers of front engine Daimler double-deckers to the Stagecoach operation in Malawi. It is unlikely that this bus ever reached Kenya.

Below: One of the Volvo B10M/Alexander buses with which Stagecoach started running services in Hong Kong. The Group had high hopes of winning further business under the tendering system in what was then a British Crown Colony, but they came to nothing.

Bottom: A team of drivers in Stagecoach uniforms in the short-lived Hong Kong operation.

would be off the road and there would be a severe shortage of public transport. She told him frankly that the port officials were demanding bribes. The President picked up a telephone, spoke in his native language, then turned to advise Ann that she would have no more trouble. It was an act of almost incredible naivety on Ann's part, but it worked.

On one of her visits to Kenya Ann was accompanied by Ewan Brown, because there was a need for a second Main Board director to be present. He found it a surreal experience and was astonished by the large numbers of small pirate minibuses — *matatus* — competing with Stagecoach. He was also impressed with the pride of the people, noticing that everyone was in a clean white shirt.

In the early 1990s Hong Kong was still a British Crown colony, due to be handed back to China in 1997. It was also (and still is) home to one of the world's most intensive networks of bus services, and in 1992 Stagecoach Hong Kong was formed to tender for some of these. The company was encouraged by the Government, which was dissatisfied with standards at one of the two major franchised operators, the old-established China Motor Bus. Stagecoach eventually started services in Hong Kong in 1994 with five Volvo B10M single-deckers and six tri-axle Olympian double-deckers, all bodied by

Alexander. The company made many attempts to expand the business through the tendering procedure, but without success, and eventually sold its Hong Kong operations in 1996.

All the senior management team at Stagecoach were travelling very regularly, and some of the schedules were particularly punishing. Neil Renilson recalls dropping Brian at Edinburgh Airport one Monday afternoon so that he could go to a meeting in Hong Kong that was likely to last around two hours. His flight departed from London in the early evening, arriving in Hong Kong the following afternoon, because of the time difference. Brian must have caught a return flight late that evening, arriving in London at the crack of dawn, because Neil picked him up to take him to a conference in Edinburgh, where he was to be one of the speakers, on the Wednesday morning!

Ribble, bought in April 1989, held a minority share in National Transport Tokens, which company had been formed to make and distribute tokens used for concessionary travel. David Graham, Director General of Greater Manchester PTE, approached Brian and proposed that they should jointly buy out NTT. Stagecoach bought a controlling interest in NTT in April 1992 and acquired the PTE's shareholding after David Graham died.

The Group still had ambitious plans for expansion within the UK but was becoming more astute in its relations with the OFT and MMC by anticipating how they might react to various proposals. The relationship with the MMC was not helped by Brian's somewhat dismissive attitude towards it. Asked on one occasion if he had read one of the MMC's reports, Brian replied that they were far too long and that he was very busy, but that Derek had read it from cover to cover . . . to which Derek had to interject to admit that he had not read said report either!

In April 1992 Magicbus, Glasgow, was sold to Kelvin Central, in a move widely seen as clearing the decks for a bid for Strathclyde Buses, which was made soon afterwards. On reflection it seems preposterous that it had to sell a 25-vehicle operation to bid for one running over 800 buses. The MMC's treatment of Stagecoach was harsh compared with that of other operators; British Bus, for instance, was able to buy a number of neighbouring companies, effectively forming a ring right round London Transport's operations, without even a hint of referral.

Left: The first venture by Stagecoach into rail operation saw two standard carriages repainted in corporate colours and attached to Aberdeen–London overnight sleeper trains. This photograph was almost certainly taken at one of the stations on the East Coast of Scotland between Dundee and Aberdeen.

Left: A Leyland Olympian of the Bluebird fleet carrying a promotional advertisement for Stagecoach Rail. Feeder services were provided by coaches into several Scottish stations. The bus behind still has to be repainted from the predominantly yellow livery that the fleet carried under Scottish Bus Group ownership.

Below: Stagecoach bought a large number of Mercedes-Benz 709D minibuses with Alexander Sprint bodywork with 25 seats in 1992/3. This bus, part of the Ribble fleet, is seen in Fleetwood in July 1996, carrying the Zippy brand that had been acquired with the services of United Transport in Preston.

Also in April 1992 Cumberland consolidated its operations in the Workington area in a building at Lillyhall that had originally been owned by Leyland National.

From the summer of 1992 British Rail planned to revise its overnight East Coast services between Aberdeen and London by running sleeper carriages only. Stagecoach thought that this would put the price of rail travel beyond the means of many passengers and negotiated a deal with British Rail for two standard carriages with full seating to be painted in Stagecoach colours and attached to the sleeper trains. Feeder coaches ran from various parts of Scotland to and from the Stagecoach Rail trains, but the business struggled. Neil Renilson feels that the rail unions interpreted it as a first step in privatisation and told all the ticket-office staff to feign ignorance as to how an intending passenger should obtain a Stagecoach Rail ticket!

With the various NBC and SBG subsidiaries Stagecoach had inherited a motley collection of minibuses. While the concept was still right for a considerable number of routes, many of the vehicles were falling due for replacement, and in May 1992 the company ordered 150 Mercedes-Benz 709D vehicles with 25-seat Alexander bodywork. The 709D was a

With the Wellington fleet came nearly 70 Volvo B58 trolleybuses with electrical equipment by the Swiss manufacturer, Brown Boveri. They had bodies built in New Zealand by Hawke and dated from 1981-6.

sturdy workhorse with a front-mounted engine and a synchromesh gearbox. All were delivered before the Euro 1 emission standards came into force in October 1993. Further large batches of these small vehicles were added subsequently, taking the total to around 1,000 within five years.

Further new buses were ordered for the African subsidiaries in May 1992. ERF built 48 chassis for Kenya Bus Services and 44 for Malawi, while DAF won an order for 12 for Kenya Bus Services.

Ever since the private placement through Noble Grossart in December 1988 Ann and Brian had planned either to repay the investors within five years or to float on the Stock Exchange. The company started to make plans for flotation.

The investment in Gray Coach Lines had been fairly disastrous. The company was strongly unionised with a lot of demarcation between jobs. Demand for coach travel had been hit by a fairly severe recession and suffered a second and more serious blow with the onset of the first Gulf War; people in North America feared terrorism and cut back dramatically on travelling. Gray Coach had a contract to run a service every 20 minutes between Toronto city centre and the airport, but ridership plunged. The company was losing money and eventually filed for protection from its creditors in July 1992. Stagecoach sold out of Canada soon after, but still managed to limit the loss on the investment to just over £1 million.

The bad experience in one Commonwealth country did not deter Stagecoach from going into another, in what has since proved to be a sound and profitable investment. In October 1992 the company bought a majority shareholding in Wellington City Transport, New Zealand, for £2.56 million. One of the interesting aspects of this transaction was that it gave Stagecoach its first experience of operating trolleybuses — a fleet of Volvos with Brown-Boveri electrical equipment, all less than 10 years old.

Interest rates were high in the UK at this time and it was difficult to do deals. Ross Martin, who still runs the New Zealand operations, had approached Stagecoach and then, before the deal was struck, bought Hutt Valley, a bus business in the Greater Wellington area, from New Zealand Railways. That, and the majority share in Wellington City Transport,

made a sound proposition. The deal brought Stagecoach into contact with MAN, which was well established in New Zealand and offered attractive deals to help modernise the fleet. Stagecoach would go on to achieve organic passenger growth for 13 years, partly because there was no fare increase in nine years, despite prices rising by a cumulative 25% in that time.

In another acquisition in October 1992 the Aldershot and Hindhead operations of Alder Valley South were bought from Q Drive and were placed under the control of Stagecoach South.

Volvo had been swamped by the order for 200 B6 midibuses and had to go to Stagecoach to explain its problems. There was some tough negotiation, because half the order was converted to B10Ms in order to meet delivery requirements, the second 100 B6s following later. The B10Ms were given 49-seat bodywork by Alexander, and most were used on a very substantial renewal of the Cumberland fleet, including taking on most of the Carlisle city services. The B10M was a very reliable product, its main drawback being the relatively high floor caused by the mid-mounted horizontal engine. Even so, it became the standard full-size single deck bus for Stagecoach for the next five years, until replaced by designs with a much lower floor.

Brian was always looking for innovative ways to grow the business and hit upon the idea of developing networks of limited-distance express services. An order was placed with Plaxton for 20 Interurban bodies, mounted on Volvo B10M chassis, the Interurban being a simplified Première coach with some bus features, such as full destination gear. They were painted in corporate colours but with Stagecoach Express fleetnames, 15 being allocated to Scotland and the others to United Counties. The most intensive network was based on Fife. Services were started between Dundee and Edinburgh, intersecting at Glenrothes with a route from St Andrews to Glasgow. It was a shrewd move, because the concessionary fare scheme in Fife permitted residents to travel outside the county's boundaries. More Volvo/Plaxton coaches were bought over the next five years to set up Express routes in several other subsidiary companies.

Preparations for flotation were continuing. Brian Cox and Barry Hinkley were appointed to the main Board. Brian Cox had extensive experience on the operations side and had risen to be Chairman of Stagecoach South and Stagecoach Rail.

By the time he joined the Board, Barry had taken over responsibility for Group Engineering. However, he retained his office in West Cumberland, and manufacturers who were failing to attend to problems could expect to be summoned to a meeting in Whitehaven, either at 9am on a Monday morning or late on a Friday afternoon! Barry had also become adept at reviewing staff structures to get the best results at competitive costs when reshaping former NBC companies.

In December 1992 Muir Russell, a senior Scottish civil servant, became a non-executive director of Stagecoach, this being the result of a Government initiative to establish closer links between the Civil Service and the business world. Ewan Brown recalls that it worked both ways, with Stagecoach benefiting from Muir Russell's input.

Ewan remembers one meeting with the Bank of Scotland in Noble Grossart's offices, just before flotation, for the annual negotiation of the bank facility. Brian, Ann and Derek represented Stagecoach. Gavin Masterton and a colleague came from the Bank, while Angus Grossart and Ewan Brown were the hosts. They had got to the coffee stage of a convivial lunch when they remembered the purpose of the meeting. The facility was extended in a couple of minutes, but two or three days would pass before anyone realised that they had not agreed the precise interest rate. And remember that Brian is and always has been teetotal!

The role of the Bank at this stage in the development of Stagecoach was very interesting. While the natural instinct of a bank is to want security, it could see the cash that the rapidly expanding business was generating. An alternative strategy to flotation was to approach the Bank to see if it would provide loan facilities of up to £100-150 million for further acquisitions. Despite the fact that Stagecoach had not used more than two thirds of the £50 million facility established in 1988, the Bank declined that proposal, but it continued to provide facilities and bought a small shareholding after flotation.

Brian speaks very highly of Ewan Brown, describing him as a co-architect of Stagecoach. He and Ann agonised over the decision of whether to go public. They still had 55% of the company and knew that it would never be the same again; on the other hand, they knew that there would be many more opportunities to acquire companies and that the money raised by flotation would enable them to do that.

Brian, Ann and Derek toured the City to drum up interest in the flotation and explained their strategy for growth. The buses of London Transport were due to be privatised, and there were around 35 PTE and municipal businesses still owned by the public sector. Privatisation of British Rail was proposed in the Conservative manifesto of 1992, and there were also likely to be further opportunities overseas. Brian talked of creating a company with a £1 billion turnover by 2000. Interestingly neither the City nor investors were in the least deterred by the OFT and MMC investigations and reports.

On 27 April 1993 Stagecoach floated on the Stock Exchange and was valued at £134 million. On offer were 33,505,954 ordinary shares at 2.5p per share. Of those, 21,778,870 had been placed by Noble Grossart with institutions prior to flotation and 11,727,084 were allocated between 44,413 public applicants. The offer to the public was over-subscribed almost eight times. Brian and Ann retained large personal shareholdings, becoming worth, on paper, £36 million and £29 million respectively. All debt with British banks was paid off at flotation.

Ewan Brown observed that Brian's conversion to being Chief Executive of a public company was absolutely perfect and that he handled the conversion

United Counties built up a network of express services using the Coachlinks brand. This Volvo B10M-62 with 51-seat Plaxton Première Interurban coachwork entered service in 1997. It is seen in June 1998 leaving Birmingham on the long route through Northampton to Corby.

The first low-floor buses ordered by Stagecoach, in 1994, were Dennis Lance SLF chassis with 40-seat bodywork built in the Netherlands by Berkhof. The frontal styling was typical of Dutch city buses of that era. East Kent 1404 (M404 OKM) is seen in Canterbury on Park & Ride work in August 1995.

Rather unusually for an ex-NBC fleet, East Kent bought quite a number of MCW Metrobus double-deckers in 1988/9. Some, including 7762 (F762 EKM), seen in Canterbury in August 1995, had high-ratio rear axles and high-back seats for longer-distance limited-stop services. This view shows the vulnerability of front domes to overhanging trees.

very well. He soon saw the benefits of going public and of being able to grow Stagecoach into a much bigger organisation.

Soon after the flotation it became known that Lancaster City Transport was interested in selling its bus operations in that city and in Morecambe. The business was squarely in Ribble territory, so Stagecoach was anxious that it should not be sold to a competitor, but it realised that the OFT was likely to reject any bid it might make. Ribble therefore registered additional services in the Lancaster area, so as to deter any potential buyer. During the bidding process Brian and Barry Hinkley met the City Council and offered to buy the depot and the newer buses in the fleet, but the offer was not accepted, and the Council continued to invite other bids. Blackpool Transport came in with a higher offer but eventually reduced it to just over £800,000. Realising that it was in a corner, the Council eventually accepted an offer from Stagecoach of £1.4 million for the depot and selected buses.

Subsequently the MMC ruled that the Stagecoach action had been against the public interest. This was, to some, an illogical decision, considering that Stagecoach had paid £600,000 more than the next-highest offer. Stagecoach was made to give the almost customary undertakings about its treatment of any new competitor that might emerge in the area.

Prices for British bus companies were steadily getting higher. Because of the MMC it was impossible to buy contiguous businesses, except for tiny fleets. Competition was coming from GRT and Badgerline (later to merge as FirstBus), British Bus, Go-Ahead and National Express.

In July 1993 Stagecoach bought East Kent Road Car Co, based in Canterbury, for £4.9 million. Another one-time NBC subsidiary, this had been bought on 5 March 1987 by a team headed by John Berkshire. Running 320 buses and coaches in eastern and southern Kent, it had expanded by buying a coach company, Marinair of Manston. East Kent was duly placed under the control of Stagecoach South.

In the same month Stagecoach sold its 50% shareholding in Hong Kong-based Speedybus Enterprises to its partner, Clement Lau, but continued to keep a watching brief on Hong Kong and China.

In August Stagecoach finally gained complete control of services in Perth when Strathtay closed its depot and withdrew its last remaining local routes, although that company still reaches Perth from Dundee and other towns in Angus.

Meanwhile Stagecoach continued with its policy of replacing elderly buses that had been acquired from NBC and SBG and were expensive to operate, and in September an order was placed for 280 Volvo chassis, comprising 110 B6 midibuses, 120 B10M single-deckers and 50 long-wheelbase Olympian double-deckers, all with Alexander bodywork. A further order, placed one month later, was for 20 B10M coaches for UTM, all to be bodied locally in Malawi by PEW. The choice of chassis was somewhat surprising, given that horizontal underfloor engines have to be treated carefully in African conditions and are highly vulnerable to flash flooding.

The Stagecoach Rail services between Scotland and London were withdrawn in October 1993, after running up losses estimated at £700,000. Competing with the variety of tickets offered by British Rail had proved difficult, but the venture did at least give the Group some valuable experience of railways. In the same month Keith Cochrane was recruited from Arthur Andersen as Group Financial Controller, at the age of 28, and soon started to play an important part in the bus team.

In November 1993 Stagecoach bought Grimsby-Cleethorpes Transport from the local council for £4.7 million. Unusually for a municipally owned company it had a substantial fleet of coaches, having bought the long-established businesses of Peter Sheffield, along with 40 vehicles, in May 1988. Managing Director of Grimsby-Cleethorpes was Les Warneford. Brian recalls that Barry Hinkley took a dislike to him because he wore a cardigan — a somewhat risky prejudice, given that the Chief Executive was (and is) renowned as a casual dresser! Les nevertheless became a key player in the bus team, running various subsidiaries and then acting as Chairman of the Midlands and North West area before taking up his current post as Managing Director, UK Bus.

A much larger acquisition came in December 1993, when Western Travel was bought for £13.75 million, bringing further former NBC subsidiaries into the Stagecoach fold. Western Travel had been formed by Mark Thomas and a number of senior and middle managers to buy the Cheltenham & Gloucester Omnibus Co, which ran a fleet of 200 vehicles in Gloucestershire and parts of Wiltshire, from NBC on 31 October 1986. On 10 December 1987 it bought Midland Red South direct from NBC, adding another

With the acquisition of Grimsby-Cleethorpes Transport in 1993 came nine unusual Dennis Lances with East Lancs EL2000 bodywork. Delivered in GCT's mainly orange livery, 5 (L705 HFU) had been repainted in Stagecoach colours by the time it was photographed in April 1998.

Bristol Omnibus Co bought several batches of relatively rare Bristol VRT double-deckers with dual-doorway bodywork and central staircases by Eastern Coach Works. By June 1997, when it was photographed in Cheltenham, 201 (JOU 160P) had lost its second door but retained the central staircase. At the time the oldest bus in the Cheltenham & Gloucester fleet, it was on a bus rally. Stagecoach subsidiaries regularly support such events.

180 vehicles and services throughout Warwickshire and north Oxfordshire, and later three or four smaller independent companies were also taken over. Meanwhile National Welsh Omnibus Services, operating a network of services in Mid and West Glamorgan and also, under the old-established Red & White name, in Monmouthshire and west Gloucestershire, had been bought from NBC by a management team on 7 May 1987. When the company went into receivership early in 1991 Western Travel bought the eastern half of the business, the Red & White operations. It also bought buses in Cynon Valley. Western Travel strengthened its position in South Wales one year later, taking a 10%

shareholding in Rhondda Buses, another company that had also taken over some of the operations of the defunct National Welsh.

More new buses were ordered in 1994, when the first of 80 MAN 11.190 buses, with bodies built in New Zealand by Designline, entered service in Wellington. In April orders were placed for 350 buses and 150 options for the British fleets and consisted of 200 Mercedes-Benz 709D, 50 B10M and 50 Olympians, all with Alexander bodywork.

Although Stagecoach had been restricted to buying only two subsidiaries in the sell-off of the Scottish Bus Group, a further company was added in June 1994.

One of the more unusual vehicles acquired by Stagecoach with the Red & White fleet was this 1991 Mercedes-Benz 709D minibus with 25-seat bodywork built by PMT. Although better known as an operator, the Potteries company built quite a number of bodies on small and medium chassis for a few years after deregulation.

Before coming into the Stagecoach Group, Midland Red South extensively rebuilt a number of Leyland Nationals, including re-powering some of them with DAF engines. With their deep, resonant exhausts they could sometimes be heard before they were seen! No 816 (BVP 816V) dated from 1980 and is seen in Coventry in October 1998.

Western Scottish had been bought by its management and employees in December 1990 and had immediately sold the northern half of its operations to Clydeside 2000 — basically what is now Arriva Scotland. Western retained Kilmarnock, Ayr, Dumfries and Galloway, with services stretching as far north as Glasgow. The price was £6 million, and another 340 buses and coaches were added to the fleet. In October of that year, Arran Transport was bought and put under the control of Western.

Just a week or two after the Western Scottish purchase Newcastle-based Busways Travel was acquired, for £27.5 million. Busways had been bought from Tyne & Wear PTE by a management/employee buy-out in March 1989 and had a fleet of 590 vehicles running services in Newcastle, Sunderland and South Shields. Meanwhile, on the other side of the world, in New Zealand, the business of Eastbourne Buses was bought, including 20 vehicles.

A further order for new buses was placed in the same month, for 50 Dennis Darts with Alexander bodywork and an option for a further 100. Dennis also secured an order for 10 of its tri-axle Dragon double-deck chassis with kit-built bodywork by Duple Metsec. Assembled by AVA in Kenya, they entered service with Stagecoach in Nairobi in an experiment to see whether high-capacity double-deckers would provide an answer to moving large numbers of people in Kenya's crowded capital. In fact the vehicles did not stand up to the heat and altitude and were later brought back to the UK for further service.

Stagecoach was keen to expand in busy urban areas that it saw as ideal bus operating territory. In July 1994 the Group bought a 20% shareholding in Sheffield-based Mainline Group (previously South Yorkshire Transport), for £900,000. In March the following year the MMC banned Stagecoach from increasing its 20% shareholding. However, Jonathan Evans, the Corporate Affairs Minister, overruled the MMC and ordered Stagecoach to sell the shareholding, because the Group already owned the neighbouring East Midland fleet, and that, he said, could lead to a reduction of competition in Sheffield. It was yet another unreasonable decision that again looked like Stagecoach-

bashing, because East Midland buses reached Sheffield from only one direction. At least Stagecoach had the satisfaction of making a profit, when the shares were sold in July 1995 to FirstBus for £2 million. First already owned Yorkshire Rider, serving Leeds, Bradford, Halifax and Huddersfield, yet there was no objection from the MMC to First's gaining such a large share of the Yorkshire bus market.

The purchase of Western Travel had included a 45% shareholding in Circle Line, Gloucester. The other 55% was bought out in August 1994, giving Stagecoach total control.

The last major step in the Government's programme to privatise public-sector bus companies had been announced towards the end of 1992, but it then took more than a year to prepare the London bus fleet for sale. The buses were divided among 10 major subsidiary companies, and bidders were prevented

With the acquisition of Midland Red South came two dozen Mercedes-Benz 811D buses with sturdy aluminium-framed bodywork by Wrights of Ballymena. They seated either 31 or 33 passengers. No 410 (J410 PRW) is seen in March 1996 on an unusual service for this type, leaving Birmingham on the X20 Express to Stratford-upon-Avon. These buses were larger, longer and more powerful than the standard Mercedes-Benz 709D models in the Stagecoach Group.

Busways Travel Services had been formed in May 1989 when a management/employee team bought the business from Tyne & Wear PTE. No 1744 (L744 VNL) was one of 15 Dennis Darts with Plaxton Pointer bodywork bought in 1993, one year before Stagecoach acquired Busways. It is seen in Newcastle in April 1996 carrying branding for the Blue Bus Services subsidiary.

With the Busways fleet came some Scania N113CRB buses with the same Alexander PS style of bodywork so popular with Stagecoach on Volvo B10M chassis. This Scania model had a vertical engine, mounted transversely at the rear, compared with the horizontal engine, mounted in mid-wheelbase, on the Volvo. No 929 (H429 EFT) was running in a remarkably peaceful Newcastle in April 1996.

Busways' Sunderland fleet included a batch of Leyland Fleetlines with Alexander bodywork with long main side windows, as seen on 835 (RCU 835S). Dating from 1977, it was therefore 19 years old when seen in Sunderland in April 1996.

Above: Initially vehicles in the Busways fleet retained their traditional colours and brands. It was not until 1995 that the fleet was gradually repainted into standard Stagecoach livery. In September 1996 637 (C637 LFT), one of 65 Leyland Olympians delivered in 1985/6 with Alexander RH bodywork, is seen outside Newcastle Central station passing an elderly Bristol RESL branded for Blue Bus Services.

Left: An immaculate Routemaster, working for the East London fleet in August 1995, one year after it was acquired by Stagecoach. The Group retained the standard London red livery, restored the cream band between the decks and topped off the effect with traditional gold fleet numbers and a gold-leaf version of the standard Stagecoach fleetname.

The East London fleet had a substantial number of Leyland Titans, dating from 1978-84. T632 (NUW 632Y) was working in Central London in July 1995 but, like many others of this type, later went on to work for other Stagecoach fleets outside the capital, usually converted to a single-door layout.

from buying more than two subsidiaries. There was, however, one important difference from the rest of the country: services in London (and Northern Ireland) would continue to be regulated. London Transport would continue to decide routes, fare levels, timetables and the type of vehicle to be used on each route. Each year approximately 20% of routes were put out to tender, and five-year contracts awarded to successful bidders, with the bus companies providing vehicles and drivers, collecting fares on behalf of the tendering authority and charging a rate per mile.

The regulated system in London does not give operators the ability to use their skills to open the market and develop new business. On the other hand, the centralised planning system of London Transport not only eliminated any wasteful competition but enabled bus services to be integrated with the Underground and suburban 'heavy rail' networks.

In September 1994 Stagecoach bid successfully for two London subsidiaries. East London Bus &

Coach was bought for £28 million and the South East London & Kent Bus Co, known as Selkent, for £14 million. East London was one of the prized companies, but Selkent was known to be a problem needing a lot of attention.

By cleverly putting the two bids together Stagecoach actually acquired East London for less than a management team had been prepared to pay. East London added 590 buses to the Group stock, and Selkent 414. The acquired vehicles included some of the earliest single-deck buses with a large part of their floor area only one step above the ground; these had Wright bodywork on Scania N113CRL chassis.

The management team at East London had been led by Roger Bowker. Although he must have been disappointed that their bid was not accepted, he stayed with Stagecoach, initially in London, later playing a very important part in the Group's activities abroad.

The acquisition trail continued in October 1994, when Cleveland Transit and Kingston-upon-Hull City

London was one of the very first operators in the UK to try out accessible buses, with the floor only one step above the ground from the front entrance to just ahead of the rear axle. The Scania N113CRL was already an established chassis, but Wrights of Ballymena, then a much smaller bodybuilder than today, was the first British bodybuilder to become involved with low-floor construction. It is a tribute to their technical capability that SLW18 (RDZ 6118) and its 15 sisters, built in 1994, were still running with the East London fleet 10 years later. This bus is seen shortly after acquisition by Stagecoach at Beckton in June 1995.

Several Leyland Lynx buses were acquired with the business of Cleveland Transit in 1994, including this late-1992 model, driven by a smartly dressed lady driver in Stockton in August 1997.

Just before selling out to Stagecoach in October 1994, Cleveland had taken delivery of 12 Volvo B10B buses with relatively rare Plaxton Verde bodywork. The B10B was effectively a rear-engined version of the B10M and was a relatively short-lived model in the UK market, soon being superseded by the B10BLE with a low floor from the front entrance to just ahead of the rear axle. No 34 (L34 HHN) is seen in Stockton in March 1996.

Right: In 1988 Kingston-upon-Hull City Transport had bought six Scania N112CRB single-deck buses with East Lancs bodywork. No 702 (F702 BAT) is seen in Halifax on a private hire in October 2001. By 2004 all had been transferred to work in Devon.

Above: The acquisition of Cleveland Transit and the Kingston-upon-Hull fleets brought several unusual makes and models into the Stagecoach Group. No 243 F143 BKH was a 1988 Dennis Dominator DDA1016 with East Lancs bodywork using Alexander screens. It was running in Hull in March 2002.

Right: Those who protested about how Stagecoach came to be the dominant operator in Darlington failed to realise the important role played by the trade union representing the drivers of the former municipal operator and did not give Stagecoach credit for investing heavily in new vehicles, replacing the elderly municipal fleet. New buses included this Volvo B6 with Plaxton Pointer bodywork, delivered to Cleveland Transit shortly before the Stagecoach takeover and seen in Darlington in April 1998.

Transport were bought for £8.36 million. Cleveland Transit had been the subject of a management/employee buy-out from its three municipal owners on Teesside in May 1991, and in December 1993 it had bought 51% of Hull, with the latter's employees holding the other 49%.

Despite the sale of Magicbus and the failure of the 1992 bid for Strathclyde Buses Brian and Neil had continued to keep a close watch on Glasgow, and in October 1994 Stagecoach Glasgow was established to operate competitive services in Scotland's largest city.

Towards the end of 1994 Stagecoach became involved in the infamous Darlington saga, which was to damage the company's reputation for some years thereafter. Since the middle of 1993 the municipally owned Darlington Transport Co had been locked in competition with United, a former NBC subsidiary, and Your Bus, a small independent company. The centre of Darlington was heavily congested, and DTC was losing money, such that the Council advertised the company for sale in July 1994. Stagecoach was already active in the North East, and its Busways subsidiary duly gave notice that it was going to start a network of services in Darlington on 12 December.

Stagecoach made an offer to buy DTC but was outbid by Yorkshire Traction, based in Barnsley and

A number of Renault S75 minibuses with 29-seat Reeve-Burgess bodywork, dating from 1990, were transferred in 1995 from Busways to the Cleveland Transit fleet. One year later J226 JJR was working in Darlington.

Cleveland Transit brought to Stagecoach quite a number of Leyland Fleetlines with Northern Counties bodywork. This 1980 model is seen when working for the Darlington subsidiary in August 1996.

another management buy-out of a former NBC subsidiary. Brian was suspicious that Yorkshire Traction intended to sell out to United, giving that operator a monopoly in Darlington.

Following an approach by the trade-union convenor at DTC, who said that his members were concerned about having to work for Yorkshire Traction and that they would prefer to join Stagecoach, the Group placed an advertisement in the local press, seeking to recruit drivers at a higher wage than DTC was paying and with the promise of a £1,000 signing-on fee. Stagecoach later argued that this would have been the cost of training a new driver. The advertisement led to the recruitment of 55 drivers, so Stagecoach registered further services, all to start on 12 December, and almost completely replicating the DTC network. Other bidders for DTC immediately withdrew their offers. Stagecoach then announced that it would run buses free of charge from 7 November until 12 December. Almost immediately DTC went into administration. Some of the newer buses were sold, and Stagecoach later bought the bus depot.

There was an outcry in the national media and the inevitable enquiry by the MMC, which called the behaviour of Stagecoach 'deplorable, predatory and against the public interest'. Labour politicians, keen to condemn the Conservatives' privatisation policy, seized on the MMC ruling, denouncing Stagecoach and accusing the OFT of being toothless. There was concern that Stagecoach could do the same with the other 20 or so companies which were still municipally owned, but Brian strenuously denied that, saying that the Darlington situation was unique.

There was nothing illegal about what happened in Darlington; one of the chief aims of the Transport Act 1985 had been to create competition in the provision of bus services. The MMC conveniently forgot that and also took scant notice of the very significant role played by the trade union. Looking back on Darlington, Ewan Brown says that it caused a disproportionate amount of flak and was even portrayed in some sections of the press as an invasion from Scotland!

In November 1994 Stagecoach bought a 20% shareholding in Strathclyde Buses for £8.3 million but was later forced to divest. Stagecoach had tried to buy the

Above: The acquisition of Hartlepool Transport brought some elderly Bristol RELL buses with Eastern Coach Works bodywork into the Stagecoach Group for a relatively short period. No 96 (JAJ 296N) is seen in its home town in March 1996.

Right: Hartlepool contributed some Dennis Falcon HC single-deckers to the Stagecoach fleet, including 31 (B31 PAJ), one of six with Northern Counties bodywork delivered in 1985, seen in Hartlepool in March 1996.

complete company from the Regional Council towards the end of 1992, but the Council eventually sold it to a management/employee buy-out in February 1993, for £30.6 million. Stagecoach complained that the price seriously undervalued the company, but Ian Lang, the Scottish Secretary, said that he had no powers to intervene.

Yet again, the MMC seemed to take a particularly hard line with Stagecoach; this time it insisted that the Group could not enter into an agreement not to compete with Strathclyde Buses! Late in 1994 Stagecoach and Strathclyde Buses both bid to buy Kelvin Central, with Strathclyde making the higher offer. Both deals were referred to the MMC, which allowed Strathclyde to keep Kelvin Central but ordered Stagecoach to divest its 20%. Yet Kelvin Central had many more buses in the Glasgow area than Stagecoach did!

If proof were required that Darlington was indeed a unique situation, Hartlepool Transport was acquired in December 1994 for £1.55 million. Bought from its municipal owner in June 1993 by its management and employees, it added 67 buses to the Group total.

In the same month the Ayrshire Bus Owners co-operative, trading as A1 Service, was bought from its members for £4.25 million. The business was merged with Western, but some of the 67 buses retained A1's attractive blue-and-cream colours. The acquisition of A1 was also referred to the MMC, but Stagecoach was allowed to keep it in exchange for behavioural undertakings.

There remained a strong relationship between Stagecoach and Volvo. The Swedish manufacturer had in Curitiba, Brazil, a factory that had developed a rapid-transit system using high-capacity articulated and bi-articulated buses, built on the B10M chassis

The rather mixed A1 Service double-deck fleet was rapidly modernised with around 20 Volvo Olympians with Alexander RL bodywork in 1995. These buses had 79 seats and were quickly put to work on trunk routes between Kilmarnock and the Ayrshire coast in the traditional A1 Service colours. No 915 (N849 VHH) is seen at Irvine in August 1997.

Among the more unusual buses inherited with the A1 Service fleet in 1995 were two Volvo B10M-56 buses with rare Duple 300 service-bus bodywork. Duple was much better known as a builder of luxury coach bodies. Western 598 (WLT 538) is seen in Irvine in August 1997.

with horizontal underfloor engine. The vehicles had a flat floor throughout, passengers getting on and off at covered platforms that were level with the floor of the bus. The first scheme was established in Curitiba itself and proved capable of moving large numbers of passengers at a fraction of the cost of a light-rail system. The city authorities in Bogota, the capital of Colombia, were interested in establishing a new mass-transit system, using 250 bi-articulated buses. Stagecoach and Volvo Bus Corporation agreed to take a 50% shareholding, the other 50% being held locally by Corporación Financiera del Transporte. The plan was to open a number of routes by converting a little-used railway into a dedicated busway, but the scheme fell through because it was difficult to get the political will to make it succeed; there were also protests from many bus drivers who feared for their livelihood. The biggest problem was a lack of transparency about procurement of the service. Stagecoach and Volvo thought there was too much revenue risk and pulled out before any investment was made, but earlier this

decade the authorities revived the concept, using dedicated bus lanes in some of the broad main avenues, with the successful introduction of the Transmileno system. Volvo supplied many of the vehicles.

The early 1990s had been an era of frenetic activity and growth, during which Brian had established the bus management team to reorganise companies quickly and deliver rapid improvements in profits. Having developed the business model, he entrusted its implementation to a team of portfolio managers, Barry Hinkley having the largest share of responsibilities, because his engineering remit covered the entire Group. Brian Cox, Tony Cox (who had joined the senior executive team) and Neil Renilson were in charge of large geographical areas of the business. It was an exciting time to be part of Stagecoach. Brian's role during this phase had become less operational, enabling him to concentrate on business development and strategy. He now started to look closely at the proposed privatisation of British Rail.

Expanding into Rail Privatisation

IN its 1992 election manifesto the Conservative Party promised to privatise British Rail, one of the few public-sector businesses still to be sold off. The then Prime Minister, John Major, is believed to have been in favour of returning to a pre-nationalisation arrangement, with four main companies based on the old Great Western, London, Midland & Scottish, London & North Eastern and Southern. However, he was talked out of that by his Minister of Transport, Malcolm Rifkind, who proposed a much more complicated arrangement that would later prove almost unworkable.

All the infrastructure — principally the track — was put into the hands of an organisation called Railtrack. Train services were divided among 25 companies, called Train Operating Companies (TOCs), plus a number of freight companies. The TOCs were awarded franchises and had to pay Railtrack for access to the lines that they needed to use. This was complicated, particularly where two or more companies required access to the same track.

All the rolling stock — locomotives, coaches and freight wagons — was divided between three rolling-stock companies (RoSCos), which leased trains to the operating companies. The rolling stock was divided in such a way that all the TOCs had to lease stock from at least two of the RoSCos. These emerged as Angel Train Contracts, Eversholt Leasing and Porterbrook Leasing. To encourage investment in new rolling stock, the RoSCos charged the same rental rates, irrespective of the age of the stock.

Ewan Brown has said that members of the financial community had looked at the RoSCos when they were first offered for sale but were worried about being overwhelmed by the risk of the cost of heavy maintenance should lots of trains need repairs. Nevertheless, it was the RoSCos that initially attracted Stagecoach. Brian had been one of the first transport people to look at them when they were originally offered for sale. They were slightly shrouded in mystery, but lurking in the middle of the terms of sale was mention of the fact that 80% of the income was guaranteed by the Government through to 2004. Even the risk of the financial collapse of a Train Operating Company was minimal, because there would still be a need to provide services, so another operator would take over almost immediately. Keith Cochrane, who worked with Brian on the Group's rail strategy, called them 'non-stick RoSCos', because there were never any liabilities that stuck to them!

Hambros had been appointed by the Government to sell the RoSCos at a time when Stagecoach had a market capitalisation of £270 million. Hambros initially started talking of around £1 billion per company, but it was in a completely new type of business, and some prospective purchasers held back because the Labour opposition was talking about re-nationalisation. That did not worry Brian. He worked with Montagu Private Equity to try to buy Angel Trains but fell about £40-50 million short of a successful bid. The combined selling price for the three RoSCos was around £1.8 billion.

A detailed prospectus was issued for every Train Operating Company, and Stagecoach asked for a copy of each. The first three rail franchises that came up for offer, in September 1995, were Great Western Trains, LTS Rail (London, Tilbury & Southend) and South West Trains. One big difference, compared with buses, was that relatively little capital was required. As already mentioned, the trains were leased, while an

One of the superb open tramcars, dating from 1903, and fully restored by Stagecoach in Portugal.

When Stagecoach acquired part of Rodoviaria de Lisboa, running services to the northwest of the Portuguese capital, the fleet was rapidly modernised with 60 Scania L113CLB buses bodied by Marcopolo. The Brazilian firm had, at that time, just established a European bodybuilding subsidiary in the city of Coimbra, north of Lisbon.

access charge was paid to Railtrack for the use of lines and stations. While the Government was keen to see innovation and improvements in services, its main priority was to reduce the level of subsidy paid to the TOCs. Some franchises were awarded on the basis that they would change over the duration of the contract from receiving a subsidy to paying for the right to run the franchise.

At the time of flotation Brian had said that part of the Stagecoach strategy for growth lay in taking part in rail privatisation. Much of 1995 was spent in preparing the rail system for this major change. Senior executives were asked to decide whether they wanted to work with Railtrack or one of the newly created TOCs. Brian, Derek and Brian Cox kept a very close watch on what was happening. In the meantime there were still opportunities to acquire further bus fleets, although Brian noticed that prices were becoming, in his words, 'toppy'. In a relatively short period prices went from around 70p per £1 of turnover to as high as £1.60. Brian would consider paying a premium only for a business that 'tucked in' to an existing part of Stagecoach. The main reason for the increase in prices was the emergence of a small number of competing groups that were keen to grow by acquisition, but another factor was the involvement of investment banks and other corporate financial advisers, the size of whose fees was linked to the sale prices achieved.

An employee buy-out had bought Chesterfield Transport from the Council in March 1990 and sold out to Stagecoach in July 1995 for £3.6 million. Although Chesterfield was in the heart of East Midland's territory the deal was accepted by the MMC as acting in the public interest — partly because Chesterfield Transport was close to becoming insolvent — and added 112 buses to the UK fleet. In a smaller transaction, in September 1995 Stagecoach bought the local bus services of the Ayrshire-based Clyde Coast co-operative, integrating them with its services in Ardrossan and putting them under the control of Western.

In August 1995 Stagecoach entered the Portuguese bus market. Much of the industry had been nationalised after the revolution of 1975, and all services outside the main cities placed under the control of Rodoviária Nacional. When the Portuguese Government decided to sell off RN this was broken into a number of subsidiaries. Stagecoach took a 25% shareholding in a joint venture with Montagu Private Equity to buy part of Rodoviária de Lisboa, running services to the north and west of Lisbon. Many of the routes served stations on the Lisbon commuter network.

The sale of the Portuguese company was conducted on the floor of the Lisbon Stock Exchange. Keith Cochrane was there in person, while Brian was at the end of a telephone in Perth. Stagecoach bought the business together with Barraquiero, a major Portuguese operator. When they later discussed division of the assets, it transpired that something had been lost in translation, because Brian thought that the deal included a trolleybus depot at Sintra. It turned out to be a 14km-long tramway, linking Sintra with the coast, with 15 vintage trams that were 100 years old! The system had fallen into disuse, but the trackbed and ancient trams survived, and in due course it was fully restored, mostly with funding from the European Union. Stagecoach had an option to buy out Montagu and would do so in January 1998, for £3 million.

As often happened when Stagecoach acquired a company, one of the first priorities was to invest in new vehicles. Portugal has a strong domestic bodybuilding industry but no chassis manufacturer. The local importers of most of the main manufacturers were asked to quote. Volvo's British subsidiary was horrified to discover later that its Portuguese counterpart had not responded to the Stagecoach enquiry, and so it was that Scania secured an order for 60 new buses bodied by Marcopolo, the major Brazilian bodybuilder that had recently established a European plant in the city of Coimbra.

Stagecoach was still wary of the workings of the MMC and therefore, in October 1995, sold its small operation in Manchester, running just 13 buses, to Finglands, a subsidiary of East Yorkshire Motor Services. This was immediately interpreted as a manoeuvre to enable Stagecoach to make an offer for Greater Manchester Buses South.

The Fife fleet acquired several batches of Stagecoach standard Volvo B10M buses with Alexander PS bodywork. Although these buses had horizontal underfloor engines, the main floor could be reached by three relatively shallow steps. The interior layout was passenger-friendly, with no internal steps. No 321 (N321 VMS) was photographed pulling out of Kirkcaldy bus station in May 1996.

In October 1995 a massive order was placed, for 1,120 new buses and coaches. The inter-urban services had proved so popular that Stagecoach decided to increase seating capacity by ordering 10 Volvo B10M articulated coaches with Plaxton bodywork. Plaxton also secured an order for 60 standard Interurban bodies on 12m B10M chassis. Northern Counties, based in Wigan, won an order for 150 bodies on Volvo Olympian chassis, while Alexander secured orders for 400 minibuses on Mercedes-Benz 709D chassis, 100 midibuses on Dennis Dart, a further 60 full-size PS single-deckers on Volvo B10M and 100 RL double-deckers on Volvo Olympian. Overseas orders included the 60 Scanias for Portugal, mentioned above, another 70 MAN for New Zealand, a further 10 Volvo B10M for Malawi and 110 ERF buses for Malawi and Kenya.

The B10M Interurbans were used by several of the British subsidiaries to introduce Stagecoach Express services, which were operated on a limited-stop basis,

attracting new customers, and became very popular. For instance, Bluebird took the Aberdeen–Inverness services to a half-hourly frequency and ran other Express routes to Fraserburgh, Peterhead and Braemar. This last route passed Balmoral Castle, and Bluebird's coaches proudly display the Royal Warrant to this day.

Managers were given the freedom to go and do the job and to try out innovative ideas. It was important to deliver financially, but if any subsidiary ran into problems, then help was quickly at hand. Neil Renilson, at the time Chairman of Stagecoach Scotland, described his job as hard work but incredibly rewarding. He recounted a story that summed up the spirit of Stagecoach. On holiday in Lanzarote, he damaged his spine and was taken to a local hospital that was unable to help him; after he had spent four or five days hooked up to a morphine drip both he and his family were getting very concerned. Ann duly hired an air ambulance that

A batch of standard long-wheelbase Volvo Olympians with Alexander RL bodywork entered service in Manchester in 1996. Their high (87-seat) capacity enabled them to cope easily with rush-hour crowds. No 726 (P726 GND) was caught in March 2000 with a Manchester tram in the background.

took him from Lanzarote to Leuchars in northeast Fife, and from there he was transferred to Stracathro Hospital in Brechin. Brian had earlier done the same for an engineer in Malawi, who was airlifted to South Africa, saving his life. When people are looked after in that manner, it engenders great loyalty.

By the mid-1990s all the main manufacturers were starting to develop buses with a large part of the floor only one step above the ground. Volvo's initial offering was the B10L, with a low floor throughout, and a 'seed' vehicle, for evaluation by the Fife fleet, was handed over to Stagecoach at the Coach & Bus exhibition in Birmingham in October 1995.

In December 1995 Stagecoach paid £12.6 million for the CHL Group (Cambus Holdings Ltd), based in Cambridge and including Viscount in Peterborough. Formed in 1984 by the division of the Eastern Counties Omnibus Co, Cambus had been the seventh NBC subsidiary to be sold, being bought by a management team led by Paul Merryweather on 5 December 1986. They had subsequently bought Premier Travel, an old-established operator of coach and stage services in the Cambridge area, and Miller's of Cambridge, and in November 1992 they had added Milton Keynes City Bus, formed in 1986 by the division of United Counties and bought from NBC by its management on 7 August 1987.

CHL added 370 buses to the Stagecoach fleet, but the Group was ordered by the MMC to divest the Milton Keynes operation, because it adjoined the territory of United Counties, and also United Counties' Huntingdon depot, because it adjoined Cambus territory. The latter was a particularly petty decision, because the Huntingdon depot had only around 25 vehicles. Milton Keynes was eventually sold to Julian Peddle; he also bought the Huntingdon operation but soon sold it on to Blazefield Holdings, a company that had been established by the management of West Yorkshire Road Car Co to take over the Harrogate-based company after it had been bought from NBC.

The CHL announcement was totally eclipsed by the news in December that Stagecoach had become the

The Royal Warrant is proudly displayed by Bluebird on the sides of some of its coaches, because the route to Braemar passes the entrance to Balmoral Castle.

Above: Volvo B10M-60 coaches with 51-seat Plaxton Première Interurban coachwork were introduced by Bluebird in 1993 to start a network of limited-stop express services in northeast Scotland. The Interurban version of the Plaxton body had a simplified interior, with fixed seats and bus-type features, like the destination gear.

Left: Nowadays classed by Stagecoach as a special-event vehicle, Viscount 52 (JAH 552D) is a 1966 Bristol FLF6G with open-top Eastern Coach Works bodywork, seen in glorious weather in Peterborough in August 2000.

The Cambus and Viscount fleets were modernised in 1996 with 52 Volvo Olympians with Northern Counties bodywork. By this time the Olympian was fitted with the Volvo 9.6-litre engine, mounted vertically and transversely at the rear, and several Volvo parts, but the design of the chassis was still pure Leyland. Viscount 546 (P546 EFL) is seen passing through the attractive town of Oundle in March 2001.

first outside company to win a rail franchise, South West Trains — the largest, by turnover, on the BR network. The initial contract was for a seven-year period, commencing 4 February 1996.

The Government was concerned that there was very little interest in the rail franchises, except from management teams. Stagecoach beat the management offer for South West Trains by a very small margin, but the Government wanted an outside bidder and Stagecoach had a much better business plan.

South West Trains ran a major network of express and suburban services from London's Waterloo station, serving more than 200 stations in South West London, Surrey, Hampshire and Dorset. Most of the trains were electric multiple-units, but there were also some Class 159 diesel units. Many of the passengers were regular commuters, and peak-hour traffic was very heavy.

Stagecoach found that the rail business was fundamentally different from buses. It was used to going into newly acquired bus companies and getting them into shape quickly; rail companies had much larger and more structured management systems, and it took quite some time to understand fully what everyone did. There were also strong trade unions and a number of quite serious restrictive practices.

The SWT franchise got off to a bad start. Stagecoach thought that there were too many drivers. The company wanted to simplify the payment system by putting them on a higher basic wage, buying-out bonus and other payments. One of the objectives was to make it easier to run services on Saturdays and Sundays.

Some drivers were offered redundancy, with the longest-serving attracting the highest payments. As it turned out a greater-than-expected number of the most widely experienced drivers took up the offer. This led to an acute shortage of drivers for several weeks, while new drivers were trained to become

familiar with each route and each type of train. Inevitably there were delays and cancellations. Stagecoach quickly found that rail passengers were much more vociferous than bus users, and there was heavy criticism in the London media. The situation also gave New Labour, under Tony Blair, a golden opportunity to criticise the Conservatives' rail-privatisation programme in the run-up to a General Election. The Conservative Party was very angry, because most of the stations on the SWT network were in its MPs' constituencies. The problems lasted for around two months, but they damaged the reputation of Stagecoach and also caused a fall in the company's share price.

Early in 1996 Stagecoach made a bid for the South Central rail franchise, jointly with a management team led by Graham Eccles. They were beaten by Connex, a subsidiary of French utility giant Compagnie Générale des Eaux. One of that company's first acts on taking over was to dismiss Graham, who joined Stagecoach the following day and thereafter, with Brian Cox, worked very hard to turn around South West Trains. Performance and reliability improved dramatically, but it would be a long time before some sections of media were placated.

If 1995 had been a busy year, it was nothing compared with what was about to happen in 1996. Events began in January, when Stagecoach paid £1.57 million for the remaining shares held by management in Wellington City Transport.

In the same month Stagecoach bought Devon General and Bayline for £16.1 million, adding 311 vehicles to the fleet. Devon General had been the first bus fleet to be bought from NBC, on 19 August 1986, by a management team of five led by Harry Blundred. They are believed to have secured the business at a very attractive price, in order to stimulate interest

Although most South West Trains stock consists of electric multiple-units, there are some diesel-powered trains for longer-distance services over non-electrified track. This Class 159 DMU, in Stagecoach corporate rail livery, was photographed passing Dawlish, on the South Devon coast, in June 2001.

The tracks outside London's Waterloo station are always heavily used. This early publicity shot was taken just after Stagecoach won the South West Trains franchise.

Harry Blundred of Devon General was a great fan of small buses that were suitable for frequent services in the narrow streets of cities like Exeter. For some vehicles he specified a front entrance and centre exit to speed passenger flow, despite the short overall length. No 467 (M249 UTM) was a Mercedes-Benz 709D with Marshall C19 bodywork, one of 20 delivered in 1995. It was running in Exeter in April 2001.

In the privatisation of NBC. They then formed a parent company, Transit Holdings, which subsequently bought South Midland, based at Witney in Oxfordshire, another former NBC subsidiary, which had been bought by two of its directors on 19 December 1986. Although most of the operations were outside Oxford, Transit Holdings started to run services in a city that Brian had coveted when he first looked at the sale of NBC companies. Transit Holdings had also bought the Portsmouth Citybus business from Stagecoach in December 1990, following instructions from Nicholas Ridley to divest. Realising that a further battle with the MMC was inevitable, Stagecoach sold the Portsmouth operation to FirstBus in March 1996.

Back in the 1980s there had been some inconsistent decisions when the large PTE companies were broken up and prepared for sale. The Greater Manchester business was divided into North and South, while the West Midlands company was allowed to be sold as one unit. In February 1996 Stagecoach bought Greater Manchester Buses South for £40.6 million, which purchase, including the small Charterplan coach fleet, added 744 vehicles.

There was considerable competition in the newly won territory, especially on the busy Wilmslow Road, serving the universities. Large numbers of students used buses in term-time. Stagecoach painted a number of older vehicles in overall blue livery and branded them 'Magic Bus', effectively in competition with its own services. The Magic Bus service ran at substantially lower fares and boosted Stagecoach's share of the traffic on the busy corridor. Magic Bus services were also operated in Glasgow and Newcastle.

Another municipal operation came into the Stagecoach sights in March 1996, when the Group bought Pendle Council's 50% shareholding in Burnley & Pendle Transport for £2 million. Stagecoach tried to persuade Burnley Council to sell its 50% shareholding, but the latter held out for several months, working in partnership with the Group.

Derek Scott now decided to step down as Finance Director to devote more time to other interests, but he remained as Company Secretary for several more years. Keith Cochrane moved up in March 1996 to replace him, having been heavily involved in acquisitions and strategy for the previous two and a half years.

The summer of 1996 was a particularly busy period, with the Group making two very significant acquisitions. In August Stagecoach made an agreed bid to take over Porterbrook Leasing, one of the privatised railway's three rolling-stock companies. Porterbrook owned 3,774 locomotives and carriages

In 1997, two Leyland Tiger coaches were transferred from Red & White to Stagecoach Devon for use on express services.
They had relatively rare Duple Laser coachwork that had been designed aerodynamically to save fuel consumption.
No 898 (AKG 197A) is seen in Exeter in August 1998.

Above: The acquisition of Greater Manchester Buses South brought a considerable number of MCW Metrobuses, including this 1983 model, seen in Manchester in October 1996 in its previous owner's colours. The Metrobuses had steel frames that were prone to corrosion whereas practically all other double-deck buses on the market were built in aluminium.

Upper left: The Stagecoach Manchester fleet was rapidly modernised with large numbers of Group-standard Volvo B10M-55 single-deckers with Alexander PS bodywork. Although the entrance steps and floor height were not ideal for intensive city services, their high passenger capacity was an asset. One of 68 new in 1996, No 852 (P852 GND) was photographed in Manchester the following April.

Lower left: Concurrently with deliveries of large numbers of high-floor B10M buses, Stagecoach Manchester bought five low-entry Volvo B10BLE models with 49-seat Northern Counties bodywork in 1997. No 604 (P604 JBU) is seen in April when almost brand-new. Much more of the structural strength of low-floor buses had to be carried at roof level, hence the deep cantrails.

Above left: The acquisition of Greater Manchester Buses South brought a batch of five Scania N113DRB buses with Northern Counties bodywork, dating from 1991. No 1467 (H467 GVM) looked immaculate in corporate livery in Ashton in October 1996.

Above right: Once production of the Leyland Atlantean ceased, the Leyland Olympian with Northern Counties bodywork became the standard double-decker in the Greater Manchester fleet. Smartly repainted into Stagecoach colours, 3117 (B117 TVU) heads through Ashton in October 1996.

Right: Stagecoach used the Magic Bus brand in several parts of its network to create services that appeared competitive with its own but also acted as a deterrent to any potential external competitor on some of the busiest routes. They operated at lower fares. Dating from 1988, Busways 690 (E919 KYR) was one of a batch of Northern Counties-bodied Leyland Olympians acquired by Busways from London Buses in 1991 and is seen here in Newcastle with a goodly number of passengers in September 1997.

— approximately one third of the country's rail stock. Stagecoach paid £475.6 million and took on debt, making the total price £825 million — by far its largest acquisition to date.

Anticipating that the deal might be referred to the MMC, because it put Stagecoach in the position of leasing rolling stock to companies with which it might compete, Stagecoach stated that it was willing to give certain assurances, including agreeing not to offer preferential prices to its own rail subsidiaries.

In a very shrewd move widely praised in the City, Stagecoach transferred £545 million of the acquisition price into bonds, secured on lease payments due to Porterbrook from Train Operating Companies. About 80% of those payments were backed by the Government, so the potential risk for bond-holders was very low, and the credit rating achieved was close to the Government's AAA.

Porterbrook was an entirely different kind of company from any previous acquisition and did not need the usual team from Perth to get it into Stage-coach shape. Although it had a large and valuable portfolio of trains, it was managed by a small team of around 30, based in Derby. It generated good monthly income streams and excellent profits and was starting to win orders from the Train Operating Companies for new rolling stock. It had originally been the subject of a management buy-out, headed by Sandy Anderson. Brian admired him greatly as an entrepreneur and the two men got on very well; there was a lot of mutual respect. Porterbrook was, in Brian's view, the best-run RoSCo, as it demonstrated by winning a lot of new business. Sandy Anderson took a considerable amount of Stagecoach stock when Porterbrook was sold and stayed on to run the business for Stagecoach.

In a second major deal, concluded just one month after the Porterbrook acquisition, Stagecoach acquired Swebus, a subsidiary of SJ (Swedish Railways). Swebus owned 3,500 buses and coaches, of which 2,900 were running in Sweden, the balance in Denmark, Finland and Norway. The price was £115.6 million in cash, with the assumption of £117 million of debt and interest, making a total of £232.6 million. The company was bought at the right price and had a turnover of £316 million. Roger Bowker moved from London to Stockholm to take charge of the new

acquisition. The Nordic countries were among the first to open bus services up to competition, and in many parts of the region there was a tendering system similar to that employed in London, so Roger's experience was very useful.

After a few months the Norwegian subsidiary, Swebus Norge AS, together with around 250 buses operating in central Norway, was sold to Norgebuss Invest AS, for £7.9 million, while control of the Finnish and Danish subsidiaries was transferred to the UK, to enable Swebus management to concentrate fully on the Swedish operations. Subsequently the Danish subsidiary was sold to the bus-operating arm of DSB (Danish State Railways), the deal involving the transfer of 140 vehicles.

Swebus was running express services, sometimes in competition with its former owner, the state-owned railway. The coaches were under-utilised, so Brian, on one of his periodic visits, suggested using them intensively, with more frequent services. It was a classic Stagecoach strategy to maximise the use of assets, and it proved to be very successful.

Roger Bowker implemented the expanded coach network and cost-reduction programmes, reporting directly to Brian. The central city of Jonköping, with motorways leading to Gothenburg, Malmo and Stockholm, was used as a hub, and the service between Gothenburg and Stockholm increased to seven departures daily. In the first year or two, traffic grew by 150%. Brian suggested that Swebus should give a discount — a special offer — on a new service. However, the instruction got mistranslated, and the discount was offered across the entire network. It was an incredibly busy summer, but it could have been more profitable!

Brian had to increase the Swebus coach fleet to meet the growing demand for express services. He talked to Volvo, which at that time worked closely with Van Hool in the Swedish market. Sitting down to negotiate with Van Hool, he first raised the matter of the unpaid invoice for the loss of use on the three

Astromega double-deckers from 1983, claiming not only the nine weeks at £300 per week but also interest accrued over the intervening 13-year period! Van Hool agreed to pay and was rewarded with a contract for 70 coaches, built to an overall length of around 13m. Before any other European country, Sweden permitted rigid vehicles longer than 12m, and Swebus also ordered some massive four-axle Neoplan Skyliner double-deckers, measuring some 15m in length.

Back home, in September 1996 the vehicles and business — but not the property — of Hyndburn Transport were bought for £660,000; Hyndburn ran services around Accrington and so fitted into Ribble's territory. Around the same time Stagecoach told Burnley Council that it intended to invest £6 million in new buses and asked the Council to contribute its half share. The Council felt unable to commit to such an investment and decided instead to sell its 50% stake for £2.85 million, giving Stagecoach total control of Burnley & Pendle Transport.

In October 1996 Stagecoach secured the franchise for the smallest system on the railway network — the

Resplendent in Porterbrook purple, Class 47 diesel-electric locomotive No 47817 stands on display at Crewe Works in April 1996. Brian Morrison

There was a time when photographers loved to pose Brian in potentially risky situations, like climbing ladders or standing on the roofs of vehicles. He is seen here on the terrace outside the Opera House in Stockholm with a new 15m four-axle double-deck coach for Swebus Express services. Sweden permitted rigid vehicles longer than 12m before any other European country.

In 1996/7 Stagecoach took delivery of 90 Volvo B6LE low-entry midibuses. Stagecoach Glasgow 375 (P375 DSA) was photographed in August 1997 leaving central Glasgow for the southern suburb of Darnley, taking advantage of the newly opened M77 motorway for a much shorter journey time.

The Island Line on the Isle of Wight is the smallest rail franchise in the UK and uses former London Underground rolling stock. Some time after Stagecoach took on the franchise, trains were repainted in a pre-historic scheme with dinosaurs. A two-car train approaches Ryde in November 2001. Note the commendable interchange between rail and bus services.

eight-mile Island Line on the Isle of Wight. Graham remembers the bid clearly. Everything was being done in a rush, and he forgot to put insurance costs into the finance model. Brian never let him forget it. However, Island Line broke even in 2002, and Stagecoach has since recouped all its losses. The trains were repainted as dinosaurs, because much of their business comes from tourists. The Island Line is a good training-ground for younger managers, because they learn all the skills of running a railway and then can progress to larger systems.

Following the enormous growth the previous year it came as no surprise that there was considerably less activity in 1997. Stagecoach had to consolidate.

In April Stagecoach Scotland started some competitive services in Glasgow, against FirstBus. These included buses that ran from the centre of the city direct to the Pollok area, using the newly opened M77 motorway. Journey times were much quicker than on

those operated by First through the city streets, and full loads were soon being carried. First retaliated in West Fife and Ayrshire, but all-out war was avoided, and the two groups have co-existed somewhat uneasily ever since.

In July Stagecoach bought the last of Harry Blundred's bus interests, comprising Oxford-based Thames Transit, the Oxford Tube, Docklands Transit (a small operation in East London) and a fleet of 120 vehicles in Queensland, Australia, used mainly on contract work.

Although Brian's first encounter with Harry Blundred had been the battle of Torquay, they subsequently became friendly. Brian admired him because he considered him to be the first NBC manager to be driven by the revenue line, and that was unusual. Harry Blundred proved consistently that he could obtain growth in provincial areas and develop new services, like the very popular Oxford Tube express

Five Dennis Lance SLF low-entry buses with Berkhof 2000 bodywork entered service with Ribble in 1996. The Lance was longer and heavier than the Dart and its floor was only one step above the ground from the front entrance until just ahead of the rear axle. No 178 (N178 LCK) is seen in Manchester in March 1998, with more Stagecoach buses in the background.

A Stagecoach standard Volvo B10M/Alexander PS picks up passengers in Coventry in June 1996, the year after it was delivered to Midland Red South. Behind it is a Leyland National that had not then been repainted into Stagecoach colours.

In January 1997 Midland Red South was running this very rare Iveco Daily 59.12 with 29-seat Alexander bodywork. It is seen in Leamington in January 1997 but migrated later that year to join many other Iveco minibuses in the Devon fleet. Standardisation on a corporate livery eliminated the need to repaint vehicles on inter-fleet transfers.

An early winter fall of snow was turning to slush in Moffat in December 1996 when Western 142 (N142 XSA), an almost-new Volvo B10M-62 with Plaxton Interurban coachwork, was photographed passing through on an express service from Dumfries to Glasgow. These coaches were used intensively by the Western subsidiary and accumulated very high mileages.

In 1996 Stagecoach bought ten articulated Volvo B10MA-55 coaches with Plaxton Première coachwork seating 71. Western 198 (P198 OSE) is seen leaving Glasgow in August 1997 on the regular express service to Ayr and Kilmarnock. Note, on either side of the destination screen, the Stagecoach logo consisting of a stylised map of the UK in Stagecoach colours.

The Alexander ALX200 body was introduced for low-entry midibuses. P497 BRS was one of nine Volvo B6LE models that entered service with Bluebird in 1996. It was working in Perth in February 1997. Note the 'LOW FLOOR' branding in traditional Stagecoach lettering at cantrail level.

One of the Group's standard Volvo B10M-55 single-deckers with Alexander PS bodywork on a low-fare service between Glasgow city centre and the large Drumchapel housing estate.

The Oxford operations included the very frequent Tube services between that city and London. Under Stagecoach ownership, they were operated by high-floor coaches, including Stagecoach Oxford 22 (J456 FSR), a 1992 Volvo B10M-60 with 46-seat Plaxton Expressliner bodywork, transferred from Midland Red South. It is seen in its home city in March 1999.

services to and from London. He ran very frequent services in Oxford, but Brian felt that minibuses were simply too small for the numbers of passengers, and Stagecoach soon introduced larger midibuses.

Bus services in Malawi were facing mounting competition from minibuses. These were becoming a problem in many parts of sub-Saharan Africa, but most governments were reluctant to control them; minibuses and pick-up trucks provided employment for large numbers of drivers and conductors. Stagecoach therefore sold its 51% stake to Admarc Investment, one of the existing minority shareholders, for a nominal consideration.

Around this time Ann began to ease up, having always promised herself that she would retire at 55. She had worked very hard, and her particular responsibilities in insurance, property and pensions had all achieved a critical mass and had become corporate functions. She remains a non-executive director.

Neil Renilson was driving into Dundee one Friday morning when Ann telephoned to ask if he would accompany her on a trip to Malawi later that day. She had re-married in 1990 and came up from London with her husband on the British Airways Shuttle to

Edinburgh, where a team of people met them in the arrivals hall. First in line was a lawyer with a number of papers that she had to sign, all marked with 'post-its'. When he was finished, the next person had some paperwork for her charitable work. Her housekeeper had come from Perth with a case of tropical clothing, and another person, from Head Office had tickets and papers that she needed for the trip. Ann disappeared into the Ladies, made a quick change, and then went with Neil to the departure lounge. The same crew was working the flight back to London, so imagine their surprise when Ann appeared in a new outfit and with another man!

In December 1997 Stagecoach became a tram operator when it was awarded a 27-year franchise to operate the Sheffield Supertram. The Group paid £1.15 million for the issued share capital of South Yorkshire Supertram Ltd and agreed to operate the system without subsidy. Also in December the shareholdings in Rhondda Buses of Arriva (as the Cowie group had now renamed itself), FirstBus (which would shortly rebrand itself FirstGroup) and Julian Peddle, together amounting to 90%, were bought for £3.8 million, giving Stagecoach total control of that business.

L719 JUD was one of an unusual batch of Dennis Darts with Plaxton Pointer bodywork seating 37 in a dual-doorway layout. Harry Blundred, Chairman of Transit Holdings, had favoured dual-door buses, to give improved passenger flow and reduce time spent at bus stops. It is seen in Oxford in March 1997, just before the Thames Transit business was acquired by Stagecoach. Along with several others of the batch, it was transferred later that year to East London.

Above: The sleek lines of the Sheffield Supertram fleet carried the Stagecoach stripes very well. Stops were at raised platforms, level with the floor of the vehicle, enabling passengers to get on and off very easily.

Left: The acquisition of the Rhondda fleet brought a great variety of buses, including three Dennis Dart SLF midibuses with Marshall Capital C39 bodywork seating 43 passengers. No 58 (P58 XBO) had entered service in 1997, just before Stagecoach took the fleet over and is seen at Barry Island on a private hire in June of that year.

Below: The acquisition of Rhondda brought into the Stagecoach fleet a pair of Mercedes-Benz O405 buses, the first ever owned. They were new in 1995 with Optare's Prisma coachwork, seating 49. No 551 (N551 MTG) had worked into Cardiff on a limited-stop service in September 2001.

In January 1998, as mentioned earlier, Stagecoach strengthened its position in Portugal by buying out Montagu Private Equity's 75% shareholding in Rodoviária de Lisboa, for £3 million. Although the City was very pleased with the performance and growth of Stagecoach, there was concern in some quarters that Brian was taking too much on his shoulders. He therefore became Executive Chairman, and Mike Kinski was appointed Chief Executive, having joined the Group as a non-executive director a few months before.

Ewan Brown is quite clear that the reason for the change in roles was not because of any pressure from the City but because Brian genuinely believed that the Group could move forward under a chief executive. Others say that Mike Kinski was seen as City-friendly. He had previously held a number of senior management positions in industry and had a reputation as a cost-cutter, with the nickname 'Killer Kinski'. Cost-cutting was hardly necessary at Stagecoach, which was already extremely lean and tightly controlled, and indeed he made three appointments to strengthen the senior management team at Group level, these being a head of IT, a Human Resources director and the first in-house head of corporate communications.

Brian devoted much of his time and energy to the strategic issues, giving Mike Kinski free rein to run the business day-to-day. This was a big change for Brian, because for years he had checked the financial reporting from each subsidiary, knowing much of the detail of their businesses and where the revenue came from.

Stagecoach was one of the darlings of the City, which was keen to see the Group become a total transportation company, by widening its horizons into other transport fields. All sorts of proposals were put to Perth — even one to make a bid for Railtrack. Nevertheless, the next acquisition still took industry observers by surprise.

Stagecoach received an approach from Matthew Hudson, owner of Prestwick Airport, who enquired whether the Group was interested in buying it. The airport, on the Ayrshire coast, has one of the longest runways in the UK and is almost always free from fog. It was a well-established base for freight traffic, particularly across the Atlantic, but scheduled passenger services had declined because of competition from Glasgow International Airport, which was much nearer the city centre. Stagecoach Aviation was duly formed in April 1998 and bought Prestwick for £41 million. Matthew Hudson took payment in Stagecoach stock and remains a shareholder to this day, with around 1% of the Group's shares. At the time of the acquisition Stagecoach Aviation stated that it planned to acquire and develop more airports in the UK and abroad. Stagecoach was not the only transport group to invest in airports around this time; National Express bought East Midlands Airport, while First acquired Bristol Airport.

Brian continued to watch developments in China with close interest. The country was opening up to foreign investment, and its industries were becoming major exporters. It had started to build a network of motorways, to take passenger traffic off the overburdened rail system, and in April 1998 Stagecoach bought a 28% holding in Road King, a toll-road operator, for £107 million.

When bidding for the various British rail franchises Stagecoach had looked at West Coast Main Line and Cross Country, but in December 1996 and February 1997 respectively those franchises were awarded, for a 15-year duration, to Richard Branson's Virgin Rail Group. It was an astute move by Virgin to bundle WCML, with its great potential, together with Cross Country, which had never made any money. After Stagecoach had looked at both franchises Virgin negotiated a risk-sharing deal with Railtrack to upgrade the West Coast line to enable trains to run at

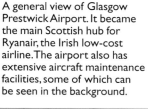

A general view of Glasgow Prestwick Airport. It became the main Scottish hub for Ryanair, the Irish low-cost airline. The airport also has extensive aircraft maintenance facilities, some of which can be seen in the background.

A number of services were operated to connect towns in the Stagecoach network with stations served by Virgin Trains. Midland Red South 8 (4828 VC), a Volvo B10M with high-floor Berkhof bodywork, is seen in Bromsgrove in June 2000 on a connecting service to Birmingham New Street station in a dedicated livery for Virgin Rail services.

140mph. In addition to renewing the track, this project needed a moving-block signalling system to control the frequent movement of high-speed trains at close intervals, but for technical reasons that system could not be developed.

The Virgin Group had floated on the London Stock Exchange in 1986 but found it an unhappy experience, pulling out and going private again within a couple of years. The Virgin Group owned 42% of Virgin Rail, the balance being held by four venture capitalists, who wanted to take their profit and were pushing the Virgin Group to float Virgin Rail.

Brian telephoned Richard Branson. They met, got on well, and agreed an alternative deal whereby Stagecoach bought out the four venture capitalists, taking a 49% investment for £108 million in cash and £50 million in Stagecoach shares. At the same time the Virgin Group increased its shareholding from 42% to 51%. The City was sceptical about the link, marking Stagecoach shares down 57p on the day of the announcement — mainly because Virgin Rail would have to turn the business around from receiving a £76.5 million subsidy in 2001/2 to returning a £220.2 million premium by 2011/12.

It was never going to be possible to straighten the West Coast main line, which had been built nearly two centuries earlier, often following contours to avoid expensive civil engineering. Although, some years before, British Rail had tried to develop tilting trains, these were not successful. However, in the intervening period Fiat had developed its 'Pendolino', having been able to make the tilting mechanism work efficiently and in a way that did not make passengers feel queasy, so Virgin ordered 53 electrically powered 'Pendolino' trainsets, to be assembled in Birmingham by Alstom. Cross Country trains used long stretches of electrified line but also non-electrified track, for which diesel power was required. An order was therefore placed with Bombardier for the supply of 78 'Voyager' trainsets. The combined value of the two orders was around £1 billion, and when delivered the new trains replaced all existing Virgin Rail stock.

Because of the massive investment in new trains, the Rail Regulator did not impose any onerous conditions on the Stagecoach/Virgin tie-up, but the OFT did. Its main requirement was that Stagecoach and Virgin should introduce a number of coach links to selected main-line stations and that more bus routes should serve stations on the two rail franchises.

The Stagecoach name was not associated with Virgin Rail in the eyes of the travelling public. Virgin had inherited old rolling stock — hence the decision to replace all of it — but was also bedevilled by the fact that most of its services ran through busy hubs, while Railtrack was hopelessly inefficient, resulting in many delays to Virgin Rail services. As Stagecoach had found out with South West Trains, rail passengers paying premium fares are not slow to protest if services do not run on time.

By this time Porterbrook had secured almost two thirds of the orders for new trains placed since privatisation. Meanwhile the two other RoSCos — Angel Train Contracts and Eversholt Leasing — had been sold to the Royal Bank of Scotland and HSBC respectively, so Stagecoach started talking to potential

Two of the best-known names in British transport, Richard Branson and Brian Souter, enter into the Christmas spirit at one of the early promotions for Virgin Rail. Both can be very humorous!

The 20 Dennis Dragon DDA1820 buses with Duple Metsec/AVA bodywork, built in 1995/6 for Stagecoach Kenya, were repatriated four years later. M683 TDB was prepared for Magic Bus services in Manchester, in this overall blue paint scheme, with no indication of Stagecoach ownership. It is seen in a damp Manchester in April 1999.

financial partners that would have the ability to raise finance at the same rates as its competitors.

August 1998 saw further expansion in New Zealand when Stagecoach bought Yellow Bus of Auckland, for £37 million. Stagecoach beat FirstGroup, which had also been interested in buying Yellow Bus, and immediately acted to bring down the average age of the fleet by ordering 60 low-floor MAN buses. At the same time, £2 million was spent on a 52% shareholding in Fullers Group, the principal ferry operator in Auckland. These transactions made Stagecoach the largest bus operator in New Zealand and, for the first time, took the Group into water-borne transport.

The bus operations in Kenya were running into political problems similar to those that had prompted the Group's departure from Malawi. Road conditions were deteriorating, and there was intensive unlicensed competition. In October 1998 Stagecoach therefore sold its 95% shareholding in its Kenyan operations to a management-led consortium for around £3 million but retained the properties and rented them to the new owners.

The 20 Dennis Dragon double-deckers that had been working in Nairobi returned to Britain in the autumn of 1998. Their bodies were strengthened (to repair the damage caused by extreme road conditions in Nairobi), heating systems installed, and their Gardner engines replaced by Cummins L10 units. They entered service on the Magic Bus routes in Manchester, where their high seating capacity was very welcome during university term-time.

Stagecoach became a ferry operator for the first time with the acquisition of a majority shareholding in Fullers Group of Auckland.

Among the last Mercedes-Benz minibuses bought by Stagecoach were 40 Vario O814 models with Alexander ALX100 bodywork, seating 29 passengers. The Vario was longer than the standard Stagecoach 709D and had a more powerful engine, developing 140bhp. Stagecoach Devon 114 (R114 NTA) is seen in Exeter in August 1998 when almost new.

Some of the subsidiaries of Stagecoach applied EasyRider or LoLiner brand names to their low-entry buses, including this Dennis Dart SLF with Alexander ALX200 bodywork, seen with the Swindon fleet in February 1998.

The Rhondda fleet was modernised in 1998 with a batch of Dennis Dart SLF low-entry models carrying Alexander ALX200 bodies. This was another fleet that used the LoLiner brand-name on accessible buses. No 621 (R621 SWO) was photographed leaving Cardiff in December 2001.

In 1998 six Dennis Dart SLF buses with Alexander ALX200 bodywork were allocated to the Nuneaton depot of Midland Red South, specially branded for the Coventry–Atherstone route. No 151 (R151 CRW) was leaving Nuneaton bus station in June 2001.

Stagecoach was relatively cautious about the introduction of low-entry buses. This was one of 22 Volvo B10BLE buses with Alexander ALX300 bodywork that joined the Busways fleet in 1997/8. The horizontal 9.6-litre engine was the same as fitted in the Group's hundreds of B10M models but was mounted in line behind the rear axle. No 2258 (R258 KRG) is seen in Newcastle when almost new in December 1998, carrying the LoLiner brand-name used for accessible buses.

The standard low-entry heavy-duty single-deck bus in the Stagecoach Group became the MAN 18.220 with Alexander ALX300 bodywork. MAN's designation denoted a vehicle designed for 18 tonnes gross, with a 220bhp engine; this was mounted vertically in line at the rear, driving through a fully automatic gearbox into a conventional rear axle. Seats above and behind the rear axle were reached by two internal steps. Compare the heights of the tops of seats in the front and rear sections in the vehicle. Stagecoach Oxford 938 (S938 CFC) is seen in Oxford in March 1999 with branding for the frequent services to Blackbird Leys.

One of 56 MAN 18.220 low-entry single-deckers with Alexander ALX300 bodywork delivered to the Group that year, Stagecoach Manchester 128 (S128 TRJ) is seen in Manchester in July 1999. The engine on these buses was mounted vertically in line at the rear, practically under the rearmost row of seats.

This Volvo B10M-62 with 51-seat Jonckheere Modulo coachwork was running on an East Midland express service to Doncaster when seen in Mansfield in May 2000. No 670 (S670 RWJ) was new in 1998, the year in which Jonckheere cornered Stagecoach orders for coachwork.

In 1998 Stagecoach bought a number of Jonckheere Mistral coach bodies on Volvo B10M-62 chassis for use on National Express work. The Mistral was built to an overall height of 3.5m with 49 seats and a toilet. Viscount 459 (S459 BCE) is seen departing from Peterborough in July 2000.

Several Citybus vehicles, in their distinctive red and yellow livery, can be seen in this busy view in Hong Kong. Note also the tram in the background.

million plus net debt of around £95.5 million. Citybus had a fleet of nearly 1,200 vehicles, most of them double-deck, with an average age of only 3.2 years. Most were Volvo Olympians with Alexander bodywork, and all were air-conditioned. In May the Group followed this by purchasing, for £2.02 million, a 45% shareholding in Hong Kong Kwoon Chung (Chongqing) Bus Investment, which company operated nearly 600 buses in Chongqing, in southwest China.

In 1999 Stagecoach invested £5.5 million in 27 new accessible low-floor double-deck coaches for the Oxford Tube service between London and Oxford. They were based on MAN chassis with a 350bhp engine mounted vertically in line at the rear. The luxuriously equipped bodies were built in Belgium by Jonckheere, which also supplied some single-deck models around the same time for Stagecoach Express services. The Oxford vehicles had 68 reclining seats, full air-conditioning, double glazing, toilets, hot/cold drinks machines and a GPS tracking system, enabling controllers to know where they were at any time. A position for a passenger in a wheelchair was fitted on eight of the 27 vehicles. The Oxford Tube had 88 departures daily, with vehicles running as frequently as every 12 minutes for much of the day.

Around the same time Stagecoach invested £1 million in an Open Learning scheme to enable staff throughout the UK to learn modern languages and improve their computer skills. It was intended to help with staff retention and recruitment and to enable the company to manage changing work practices. Available to employees 24 hours a day, the first centre was opened at Waterloo station.

Stagecoach looked next at opportunities to buy into the Italian market. Bus services in most cities were tightly controlled by the municipalities, but there was a large network of inter-urban services that were opening up to competitive tendering. In June 1999 Stagecoach stated that it planned to buy 35% of Sogin Group, the largest privately managed bus/coach company in Italy, from the Vinella family, which held 45%; the other 55% of Sogin, which ran approximately 1,800 buses and coaches, was owned by the Italian State Railways. There were suggestions that Stagecoach could increase its holding to 45%, and even that the State Railways might be willing to sell its share. A price of around £23.5 million was discussed for the initial 35% stake, but although negotiations continued for some time it was eventually announced, towards the end of the year, that the parties had failed to agree on a valuation. Stagecoach also found it difficult to assess who had control of the business.

In the meantime Mike Kinski took over the Chairmanship of Swebus, because the company was going through a rather turbulent period. Tender prices were linked to a consumer price index that actually went down during periods of deflation in the Swedish economy, while the company was also locked into wage increases that had been negotiated by the previous owner, Swedish Railways. There was strong competition for contracts, with frequent changes, especially in cities like Stockholm. The inter-urban Swebus Express operations were making a positive contribution, but the overall results were not reaching the level that Stagecoach normally expected to achieve.

The major British bus groups realised that there was little scope for expansion or amalgamation in the UK,

In the autumn of 1998 the British bus operations were restructured into three new business areas under the chairmanship of Barry Hinkley. Malcolm Howitt took responsibility for Scotland and the North East, Les Warneford took on the Midlands and North West and Tony Cox took charge of London and the South. Each had around 2,400-3,000 vehicles under his control. The reorganisation led to the departure of some long-serving executives, most notably Neil Renilson and Tony Cox (although Tony would later rejoin the Group). Meanwhile Graham Eccles took over as Managing Director of the Rail Division from Brian Cox, who became Group Commercial Director but continued to chair the SWT Board; he was also given a brief to develop integrated transport opportunities within the Group.

After the earlier failure to gain a share of the action in Hong Kong, Stagecoach bought Citybus from the CNT group in January 1999. The price was £180

because the MMC would inevitably block any acquisition that would create a monopoly in a significant part of the country. Furthermore, the rail network had been privatised, and there would be no opportunity for growth until franchises came up for renewal. Stagecoach and the other big British groups thus had to look abroad for growth. In 1998 National Express had gone into the school-bus business in the United States. The provision of school-bus services was (and is) a very large business in

North America; although many of the vehicles were owned by public authorities there was a growing trend to outsource the work to private contractors, and National Express saw an opportunity for growth, which was achieved in a series of acquisitions.

North America seemed to be the potential area for growth, and in June 1999, its executive team having thoroughly investigated the opportunities for acquisition and expansion, Stagecoach crossed the Atlantic and struck its largest-ever deal.

Above: In 1999, Stagecoach transformed the very frequent Oxford Tube services to and from London by investing in 27 MAN 24.350 tri-axle double-deckers with Jonckheere Monaco coachwork. They seated 53 on the upper deck and 15 downstairs in considerable comfort. They had reclining seats and belts, full air conditioning and tinted double glazed windows. Services ran round the clock, as frequently as every ten minutes in peak periods. This coach is seen when nearly new in London in July 1999. When replaced by new and larger Neoplan double-deckers in 2004, these coaches were dispersed to other parts of the Stagecoach Group for further service.

Left: Stagecoach has always encouraged its staff to gain additional qualifications. Here a group of staff at Busways proudly display newly won NVQ certificates.

Above: Further batches of Volvo Olympians entered service with the London fleets in 1997 like VN116 (R116 XNO), in 1998. By 2004 this bus had been transferred to Bluebird, because the London operations were by that time moving almost wholly to low-floor buses.

Right: Stagecoach invested heavily in Volvo Olympians for the East London fleet in the period 1996-8, displacing many Leyland Titans that still had plenty of life in them. Many believe that the Titan was the best driver's double-decker ever produced. One-time T664 (NUW 664Y) was one of several transferred to the Transit fleet in 1997 and was photographed in Stockton in April 1999.

A Stagecoach bus that isn't. In the late 1990s a number of Barton vehicles were painted in Stagecoach livery for use on service 757 between Mansfield and Nottingham, worked jointly with East Midland. A Barton DAF SB220/Optare Delta is seen leaving Mansfield in May 2000.

Above: Jonckheere supplied six articulated Modulo Interurban coaches to Stagecoach in 1999 on Volvo B10MA-55 chassis. They seated 72 and some, including Kingston-upon-Hull 97 (T97 JHN), went to work on express services between Hull and Sheffield. The fixed trailer axle had twin rear tyres. While that gave a better ride than a steerable axle with single tyres, the downside was a slight increase in tyre wear when turning. This coach is seen in Birmingham on a private hire when almost new.

Left: Dennis rapidly developed the Trident low-floor double-deck chassis, to meet demand from London and other parts of the United Kingdom for fully accessible double-deck buses. Alexander designed its ALX400 body for the new generation of chassis. TA61 (T661 KPU) was one of the first order for 100 buses and is seen in London when nearly new. While many of this first batch were transferred to other Stagecoach fleets, this one was still running in London in 2004.

Calamity then Recovery

Keith Cochrane *(left)*, Brian and Martin Griffiths *(right)* in a publicity shot at the time of the acquisition of Coach USA. The sharp-eyed will spot that the vehicle alongside Keith was a Volvo B10M with Plaxton coachwork that was temporarily repainted on its nearside for this promotion.

STAGECOACH was not attracted to the North American school-bus sector, having decided that it was not the kind of business that the Group wanted to enter. The executive team found another prospect that seemed more appealing, Coach USA, the largest operator of motor-coach services in the United States. Apart from the struggling Greyhound express network (not part of Coach USA), much of the coach industry was highly fragmented and mainly family-owned.

Coach USA had been founded only in September 1995 and had raised money for expansion with an initial public offering in May 1996, at which time Stagecoach executives had first met the principals of Coach USA. The company started to grow by purchasing coach businesses all across the United States, as well as in Canada and Puerto Rico. The pace was rapid, some 71 companies, representing $450 million of revenue, being acquired between the Initial Public Offering and the end of 1998. In that short period of time Coach USA had become the largest US provider of motor-coach charter, tours and sightseeing services, but it still had less than 4% of the total market.

In June 1999 Stagecoach agreed to buy Coach USA. The price was £773 million plus net debt of £357 million, making a total of £1,130 million (the exchange rate at that time being $1.58=£1.00). There was concern that Stagecoach had apparently paid a huge amount for goodwill, because the net assets of Coach USA were worth only £218 million, and there were even suggestions that US financial institutions had turned the company down when it asked for more money for expansion. It also emerged that FirstGroup and National Express had both been courting Coach USA and that Stagecoach pipped the Aberdeen-based group to the post by a very narrow margin. Larry King, the Chief Executive, joined the main board of Stagecoach.

Coach USA operated 4,500 full-size motor coaches and 2,000 minibuses, school buses and vans, with an average age of less than five years. It also owned and operated 120 garages providing maintenance services to the fleet and had despatching and related services for a fleet of 3,300 taxis. Revenue was split 41% in the North East, 22% West, 11% South Central, 9% South East, 11% North Central and 6% Canada. Operations were based in 33 US states and two Canadian provinces. Coach USA operated in 23 of the 25 cities that were the leading centres for conventions and other attractions that generated business for coaches.

Stagecoach stated that the acquisition of Coach USA offered significant opportunities for organic growth and the prospect of a position as the leading consolidator in a US industry that was expected to grow at approximately 6% per annum, due to favourable trends and demographics. There were three main types of motor-coach service — recreation/excursion, commuter/transit and regular scheduled inter-city services. Coach USA reckoned that the industry was still highly fragmented; around 5,000 operators were active in a market that had revenues in 1998 of around $12.5 billion. There was similar fragmentation in the provision of airport, ground-transportation, taxi-cab and paratransit (welfare) services, this market representing over $3 billion of potential revenues annually. Approximately two thirds of the US school-bus industry, which brought in around $9.5 billion in 1998, remained in state ownership. Looking at the scale of opportunities, Coach USA reckoned that there were 35 potential acquisitions with an annual revenue base greater than $12.5 million, 70 with a revenue base of $6-12 million and 135 with a base of $3-6 million.

Stagecoach was also attracted to the growing privatisation of services. There were opportunities for substantial economies of scale and to create a national company, and consolidation opportunities were available at a reasonable price. Before the end of 1999 Coach USA paid $106 million (£67.3 million) for a further 11 coach and/or taxi companies throughout the United States, adding a further 1,000 vehicles. Stagecoach negotiated a £1.45 billion loan facility with the Bank of Scotland, the Royal Bank of Scotland, Crédit Suisse, First Boston and JP Morgan to fund the acquisition. Part was used to re-finance Coach USA, and some was available for further acquisitions in the United States.

Back in the UK, practically every local service bus was one-man-operated, the main exception being London's Routemasters. However, journey times were increased by the need for drivers to collect fares and check multi-journey tickets. The worst time was Monday morning, when regular passengers bought their weekly tickets. The most promising solution to this problem was the 'smart card'. Similar to a credit card but designed principally for use on public transport, it could be read by a scanner that would automatically deduct the cost of each journey. Passengers would be advised on an adjacent monitor if they were getting low on credit.

Stagecoach had already started to prepare for smart cards by installing a large number of new electronic fare-collection systems in their buses in the UK. Although these continued to use paper tickets, the system was capable of being upgraded to accept contact-less smart cards. It was planned to have this equipment on all the UK bus fleet within two to three years.

In October 1999 Stagecoach bought a 20% share in Prepayment Cards Ltd, a business founded by the Australian smart-card developer, ERG. The latter retained a 70% stake, while IT specialist Sema Group had 10%. The partners intended to market smart-card technology in the British passenger transport industry. Stagecoach paid £8 million for its shareholding. Subsequently FirstGroup bought 20% and National Express 10% of Prepayment Cards from ERG. That made sense, and not just because there were places where the activities of the bus operating groups overlapped. Stagecoach already had practical experience of Octopus smart cards through its Hong Kong Citybus subsidiary.

In practice the use of smart cards has developed much more slowly than expected, and the cards' unique chips are quite expensive. Les Warneford is far from persuaded for the need. He can understand local authorities' wanting to capture some of the data but cannot see a real benefit for British bus operations.

In October 1999 Stagecoach sold Swebus to Concordia Bus, a subsidiary of the Schoyens Group, a transport and investment company based in Oslo, Norway, backed by a private equity fund associated with Goldman Sachs. A combination of factors led to this decision. Margins had become poorer because levels of subsidy were tied to an inflation index, but Sweden went through a period of deflation, which had never been expected to last as long as it did. Despite a dramatic increase in express coach travel, some tenders had been lost, and the strength of sterling against the Swedish Krona was not helpful.

Stagecoach received £203.5 million for Swebus, amounting to a loss of £12.3 million. However, the timing of the sale later proved to be absolutely right, because it was followed by even more intense competition between contractors in the Swedish market, especially in the Stockholm area. One company went bankrupt, and Concordia made a series of annual losses.

Stagecoach inherited many coaches built by Motor Coach Industries, the largest builder of commuter and charter coaches in North America, and has since placed orders for new coaches with the Winnipeg-based manufacturer.

In the same month Stagecoach launched a re-financing strategy to help pay for Coach USA and said that it could lead to a New York Stock Market listing. The Group went on a global road show in 1999 to promote an International Offering of shares, believed to be the first of its kind seen on the London Stock Exchange.

Shareholders bid for stocks at a range of prices, then, after a closing date, had to wait for around a week before being advised of the quantity of shares to be issued and the price. Brian and Ann (and their respective trusts) undertook not to apply for any application under the open offer. The concept of making sealed bids for new shares was not unknown on world markets, but it was relatively new to UK investors, who were much more used to being offered rights issues to increase capital.

Stagecoach shares stood at around 200p at this time. Analysts suggested that a rights issue at that time would have been priced at around 170-180p. There was, however, a disappointing lack of interest in the new offer at such prices or higher, so that, when the placing price was finally announced, it was set at 154p — a substantial discount.

Although traffic congestion was getting worse in most British towns and cities, bus companies still found it difficult to persuade motorists to leave their cars at home and travel by bus. Part of the problem was the poor public perception of buses, especially by those who did not use them. A number of cities proposed building tramways, but the costs were prohibitive, unless there was a high level of subsidy from central or local government, as in Manchester and Sheffield, and there was also enormous disruption during the construction period.

A less expensive option was the bus-based rapid-transit system, using its own dedicated roadway. A developer, Rapid Transit International, proposed building a rapid-transit system in Northampton. It was expected to cost £50 million and there were plans to operate up to 60 gas-fuelled vehicles, with very low exhaust emissions, on six main corridors.

Some of the cost was to be contributed by developers of adjacent new housing. Towards the end of 1999 Stagecoach was named as the preferred operator. Three months later, the Group acquired a 50% share in the scheme, with the other 50% held by Galliford PLC, a large construction company. The partners not only proposed to build the system in Northampton but also formed a joint company, RTI Stagecoach Ltd, to promote rapid transit in other locations. Cambridge, already served by Stagecoach, was one of the first targets.

In October 1999 Stagecoach announced plans to spend a further £550 million to expand in North America, having amassed a war chest for the purpose. However, even at this stage, Brian, as Executive Chairman, was coming to the conclusion that Stagecoach had made the biggest mistake of its corporate career in the purchase of Coach USA; he felt that it was not properly consolidated and was not being properly managed.

Arthur Andersen, Houston, had carried out due diligence on behalf of Stagecoach and had also audited Coach USA's 1998 financial statements. A number of irregularities in pre-acquisition accounting at Coach USA were later discovered by Stagecoach, and Brian was put in the difficult position of considering litigation against his own former employer from the late 1970s. However, the Board decided against such action. (Following the later Enron scandal, in which the same Houston office of Andersen was so deeply implicated that the international accountancy group collapsed, the potential conflict of interests of employing former auditors would not now be possible.)

Brian's instinct was to cut and run from some parts of the business but to keep the parts that Stagecoach liked. As Executive Chairman he was only in an advisory position. Talking to him, one can sense that he was deeply unhappy about being able to give advice but unable to act. The City was losing confidence, and the share price was falling steeply. Something had to give, and in February 2000 Mike Kinski resigned.

Stagecoach had lost some loyal and experienced people. Others kept their heads down, but it must have become clear to Brian and the Board that Mike Kinski was losing the support of his senior executives. He deserves a modicum of defence; although Stagecoach was a public limited company, there was still a lot of family loyalty to Brian (Ann having by this time retired).

Mike Kinski made few friends in Stagecoach. He did not come in without any understanding of how it worked, having served for several months as a non-executive director and, with the benefit of hindsight, he should have better judged the culture of Stagecoach. Despite a good working relationship between Brian and Mike Kinski, there was a clash in style; Brian was a strategist and willing to take risks, within calculated parameters, while Mike Kinski was said by some to have been totally risk-averse and obsessed with margins. Brian is more forgiving than others in Stagecoach about this interlude. Tactfully, in one interview he said that the Group thinks long and hard before bringing in any senior person from outside, and he also regretted losing people like Tony Cox, who has since rejoined, and Neil Renilson, who has since made a successful career at Lothian Buses.

Almost at the same time, it was announced that Larry King would leave Coach USA and resign from the Stagecoach Board. His co-founder, Frank Gallagher, took his place at Coach USA. Linda Bell, Director of Financial Control at Perth, moved across the Atlantic to become the Chief Financial Officer of Coach USA, effectively taking over from King.

Keith Cochrane, who had been with the Group since 1993 and fully understood the way that it was run, stepped up to become Chief Executive. He may have lacked Brian's charisma and communication skills, but he was widely respected in the City and by the Group's bankers as a very able Finance Director. Everyone saw him as being on a much closer wavelength with Brian.

Stagecoach had increased its borrowings to acquire Coach USA and wanted to reduce debt. In March 2000

For low-floor double-deck buses in provincial fleets Stagecoach standardised on the 10.5m-long Dennis Trident with Alexander ALX400 bodywork. The normal layout was 51 seats on the upper deck with 28 and a single doorway on the lower deck. Large numbers have entered service with Stagecoach Manchester. No 636 (W636 RND) is seen in the city centre in March 2000. Note the promotion of a seven-day ticket for only £3.50. The Stagecoach vehicle is passing a single-decker of Dennis's, a company that Stagecoach would buy in April 2005.

Although most Dennis Darts in the Stagecoach Group, especially outside London, are 10.7m long, there are a few of the longer SPD models, built to 11.3m. They include East Midland 837 (X837 AKW), new in 2000 with Plaxton Pointer bodywork and seen in Mansfield in April 2002.

the Group sold Porterbrook to Abbey National for £773 million and the assumption by Abbey of £669 million external debt and train-purchase commitments. Banks had by this time become much more comfortable with the RoSCos.

Stagecoach realised that around 60% of Britain's rolling stock needed to be replaced. That would require access to enormous funds, and it was becoming obvious that all three RoSCos would end up being owned by banks. Stagecoach had previously looked at a deal to buy Angel Trains but was concerned that the MMC would intervene. The Group had passed on its knowledge of RoSCos to the Royal Bank of Scotland, which went on to buy Angel Trains.

The sale of Porterbrook made a profit of £115 million. While the Group had placed orders for new trains it had not written any cheques for them. Stagecoach also got out of the business before any uncertainty that might arise with the end of the Government's train-rental guarantees in 2004.

In Hong Kong operators were given a licence for each vehicle operated, but the overall number was controlled — a major incentive to run maximum-capacity double-deck buses, almost around the clock. Late in 1999 Stagecoach brought back from Citybus a batch of 21 air-conditioned Plaxton-bodied Dennis Darts, which, following refurbishment, were placed in service in Devon and Portsmouth.

In June 2000 Ribble bought the former MTL operation at Heysham, on the Lancashire coast, from Arriva North West, giving its Cumberland subsidiary a strong position in the Lancaster/Morecambe area.

Although Coach USA acquired further companies in the United States in 2000, Brian now fully realised that Stagecoach had bought a business with some seriously under-performing parts; there were so many different types of businesses, all across the United States and Canada. Bill Luke, founder and former publisher of *Bus Ride*, the leading North American magazine for the bus and coach industry, feels that Stagecoach failed to understand the completely different nature of coach operations and the quite different culture. Linda Bell introduced tighter controls and strict reporting disciplines, while Keith found that he was also spending an increasing amount of his time across the Atlantic.

The City was not at all impressed by the problems at Coach USA. Over a two-day period in April 2000 the share price fell from 121.5p to 56.5p, reducing the market capitalisation of the Group to only £935 million. The jitters extended to other transport groups, which all saw their values fall by around 20%.

In July 2000 Stagecoach decided to bring all its senior management functions together at the Perth headquarters. Graham Eccles became Director for Rail Operations and also took on responsibility for Health & Safety issues across the Group. Andrew Haines replaced him as Managing Director of South West Trains. Barry Hinkley had resigned, Brian Cox taking his place as Managing Director of UK Bus and transferring his remaining rail responsibilities to Graham.

When Stagecoach acquired Citybus in Hong Kong, the fleet had 21 9.8m-long Dennis Darts with Plaxton Pointer bodywork, seating 39. They were replaced by new double-deckers and were brought back from Hong Kong in 1999, including Stagecoach Devon 743 (N743 XDV), seen in Dawlish in March 2000. The air conditioning unit, seen on top of the roof, must be welcome in Devon summers.

Later in the year Stagecoach launched a nationwide marketing campaign, called 'Fuelsaver', by which it intended to grow revenue. Posters and leaflets were circulated throughout the bus network, outside London, encouraging motorists to check the latest bargain fares at a time when fuel prices were rising sharply. The campaign focused on the Megarider weekly ticket that allowed the user unlimited bus travel.

Towards the end of the year Stagecoach launched a new livery for its UK bus fleet. The new livery was designed by Best Impressions and replaced the stripes that had been in use since 1981. The Group's London buses retained the traditional red, with the addition of orange/blue swirls and dark-blue skirt. McKinstrie Wilde of Edinburgh designed a new corporate interior that looked warmer and more welcoming.

At the beginning of 2001 Prestwick Airport was sold to an international consortium consisting of a New Zealand-based infrastructure-investment company, Infratil, a UK utilities fund, SUIT, and a Scottish investor, Omniport. More than £10 million had been invested in the airport, and passenger numbers had increased, but the largest freight operator, Federal Express, had moved out. Stagecoach had decided to pull back from being a provider of all kinds of transport systems in order to concentrate on the core bus and rail business. The sale of Prestwick raised £33.4 million and marked the withdrawal of Stagecoach from the airport sector.

In March 2001 Virgin Rail launched an ambitious bid to take over the East Coast franchise from GNER. The plans included building a new line, around 128 miles long, from Huntingdon to north of Doncaster, approximately parallel to the existing East Coast main line. It would be designed for trains capable of running at 200mph, equivalent to the speed of the French TGV, and would considerably reduce journey times between London and Leeds, York, Newcastle-upon-Tyne and Edinburgh. Other sections of the track would be upgraded for higher-speed running, and there would be investment in 55-60 very high-speed trains. The existing parallel track would be available to other operators to run trains at up to 125mph. Unfortunately, by this time, the Strategic Rail Authority was cooling to the idea of advanced railways, because of the high cost of overruns on upgrading the West Coast main line.

It was no secret that Ribble was probably Stagecoach's most poorly performing bus subsidiary. It had a difficult territory, with municipally owned operators serving towns like Blackpool, Preston and Blackburn. In March 2001 the eastern part of the company, including depots at Blackburn, Bolton, Burnley and Clitheroe, along with 232 vehicles, was sold to Blazefield Holdings for £13 million.

The Strategic Rail Authority announced in May that it had accepted South West Trains' bid to retain its franchise for a further period of up to 15 years. The company had identified capacity as a critical issue; passenger numbers had grown by 30% since Stagecoach first took on the franchise in 1996, and although more than 12,000 extra seats had been provided, overcrowding was still a problem at peak periods. SWT therefore promised to introduce a package of measures, including closed-circuit television for better passenger security at stations, and passenger lounges. The company also wanted to introduce longer trains, with up to 10 carriages, but Railtrack was unable to commit to the investment necessary to improve the infrastructure.

An important part of SWT's bid was an agreement in advance with Angel Trains to fund the purchase, if successful, of a large quantity of new trains. On the day that the franchise was renewed Stagecoach confirmed an order with Siemens for 177 sets of 'Desiro' electric multiple-units, some four-car and others five-car. This was worth just over £1 billion — the largest order ever placed in the UK for new rolling stock. Although 30 trainsets were later diverted to another franchise, the 'Desiros' were due to replace the last of the old but reliable slam-door trains in 2005.

The introduction of new trains was seriously delayed because the third-rail electricity supply on the SWT network could not provide enough power. British Rail had been a 'joined-up' railway, but after privatisation Railtrack had responsibility for the track and infrastructure. Graham said that SWT gave Railtrack the specifications of the trains that were being bought. Railtrack knew that they would use more electricity, because they were heavier, had different traction patterns, more on-board systems (like air-conditioning) that consumed power, accelerated faster and had a higher top speed than the trains that they were replacing.

Graham had joined the former British Rail as a 15-year-old and had worked his way up. Perhaps that lowly start helps to explain his direct, no-nonsense style, much like Brian's. Electricity sub-stations were located every three miles alongside the track on the SWT network, but these needed to be increased to every $1\frac{1}{2}$ miles. Railtrack, however, did nothing to upgrade the power supply. Fortunately, after being put into administration by the Government, it was succeeded by Network Rail, which Graham credits with implementing a well-managed project to increase the power supply, scheduled for completion by during 2005.

Stagecoach regularly called for control over the tracks that its trains used, although relations with Network Rail are now much better. In December 2001 Stagecoach issued a discussion paper, 'A Platform for Change', calling for vertical integration within the rail network and restoration of the close relationship between wheel and track. Specifically, the Group proposed the introduction of vertical integration on the SWT network. In typically direct style, Brian said: 'We believe in the future of Britain's railways, as

Brian Cox (left) and Keith Cochrane (right) promote the MegaRider bus pass, designed to tempt people to leave their cars at home and use public transport.

demonstrated by our orders for new trains, which will bring a step-change in passenger perception in the next few years, but these efforts will fail if we do not address the maintenance and renewal problems arising from decades of under-funding and weak management of the track. We believe this is the railway-man's solution to the problems of our railways.' Stagecoach proposed an initial five-year pilot scheme on SWT, carrying out maintenance work to reach an agreed asset condition.

The Group believed it was essential to have network control consolidated as one function. This would eliminate perverse incentives and a blame culture and result in more efficient and targeted use of asset funding. The train operator was, in its view, best placed to look after the interests of passengers.

As part of its bid to renew the SWT franchise the Group wanted to invest in the upgrading of a very heavily used 10-mile stretch of track near Waterloo by paying for high-strength rails, with electronic monitoring of points and higher-capacity track circuits to reduce the number of failures. SWT said that the cost of these improvements would be recovered from extra journeys, better train performance and reductions in fines for poor performance.

In June 2001 Stagecoach wrote down the value of Coach USA by £376 million. Brian said that trading performance at Coach USA had been disappointing, but the Group remained firmly of the view that North America still provided significant growth opportunities in the longer term.

Also in June, Stagecoach Portugal was sold to new local owners, for £14 million. Like Swebus and Prestwick Airport, it was considered a non-core business. Keith said that the Portuguese company's geographic position was no longer consistent with Group strategy, and he felt that the price represented good value for shareholders. In the same month the bus operation in Queensland, Australia, and 164 buses were sold to two local operators.

In 2001 British politicians were still interested in light-rail schemes as an alternative method of attracting people out of cars and on to public transport. Stagecoach was short-listed for a tender to design, build and operate the South Hampshire Rapid Transport, a 14km light-rail scheme connecting Portsmouth, by a tunnel under the harbour, with Gosport and Fareham. However, there was growing concern about the high capital costs of light-rail schemes, and it was not until July 2004 that the Department for Transport asked for a further review of costs and forecast revenues.

Despite the problems at Coach USA Stagecoach was still interested in running public transport in North America, and in June 2001 the Group was selected as one of the preferred bidders for a five-year contract to run the commuter rail network in Boston. However, in November Stagecoach pulled out of the final stages of bidding, because it could not reach agreement over responsibility for insurance risks.

The North American operations were dealt a further blow by the terrorist attacks of 11 September 2001. Sightseeing and commuter services in New York were halted for up to three days. Many airports were closed, but, more ominously, the short-term disruption was followed by a prolonged downturn in air travel that hit tourism and the convention industry, with a knock-on effect for Coach USA's operations, which relied on such trade in several parts of the country.

Stagecoach continued to introduce innovations on the British bus scene. The Group wanted to encourage growth in the use of buses and looked at a number of its networks. In Cambridge 40 new MAN/Alexander low-floor buses were introduced on 'Citi'-branded services, with high frequencies that encouraged passengers to turn up and travel. The citizens of Cambridge on the whole supported the new network, growth of 45% being achieved in a three-year period, despite problems with congestion in the city centre. Part of the reason for choosing Cambridge was that the population was forecast to grow to 250,000 within 10-15 years.

Stagecoach saw the Optare Solo M850 midibus, seating 26 passengers, as the ideal replacement for its high-floor Mercedes-Benz minibuses. New in 2001, this Midland Red South example was working on a local service in Leamington in October 2003. These little buses looked smart in the corporate livery and became very popular with passengers, because most of the floor was only one step above the ground.

The integral Optare Excel is a rare vehicle in Stagecoach Group fleets. East Midland 510 (YN51 VHV) was one of 16 L1180 (i.e. 11.8m-long) models delivered to that fleet in 2001. It was photographed running in a wet Rotherham in January 2002.

Deliveries to the London fleets in 2001 included 99 Dennis Tridents built to an overall length of 9.9m with Alexander ALX400 bodies to an overall height of 4.4m. TAS531 (LX51 FOT) of the Selkent fleet was photographed in Croydon in July 2002.

Looking very smart in the new corporate livery is Stagecoach Manchester 1629 (ML02 KCV), a Dennis Trident with Alexander bodywork new in 2002. Double-deck buses for service outside London are built to an overall height of 14ft 2in and also carry a substantial guard to protect the front and side glass of the upper deck from overhanging trees. This bus is seen in Manchester when almost new in May 2002.

Stagecoach also launched a new series of pocket guides giving information on bus networks in 35 of the towns and cities that it served around the UK. They had maps, fares and timetables for local networks, as well as details of connecting inter-urban services and rail links. Brian Cox said this was the biggest commitment to information provision by any bus group since deregulation and described the supply of up-to-date travel information as helping to eliminate one of the biggest single barriers to the use of buses, namely lack of information.

In February 2002 Stagecoach was nominated as the operating partner for an experiment involving fuel-cell-powered buses, due to start in Cambridge in October 2003. The project was led by Cambridge University, which had secured the promise of some European funding. The buses were due to provide a service for staff, students and visitors between the University campus, in west Cambridge, and the city centre. Unfortunately other funding failed to materialise, and the project had to be abandoned.

Early in 2002 Virgin Rail started to take delivery of its 'Voyager' trains for the Cross Country franchise, these comprising a mix of four- and five-car trainsets. There was one diesel engine in each car, with an IGBT inverter driving two three-phase electric motors. The trains had a combination of coil and air suspension. All 40 five-car trains and four of the four-car trains had a tilting mechanism, enabling them to run at up to 125mph.

Virgin Rail was also anticipating delivery later in the year of the first 'Pendolino' trains for the West Coast main line. However, it was now clear that Railtrack would be unable to upgrade the line for running at 140mph — a speed which was critical on longer routes if the WCML was to capture a significant part of the market from air travel. Virgin Rail received £90 million from Railtrack in compensation for its failure and also negotiated a further £90 million in reduced track-access charges.

The upgrading of the West Coast main line should have cost £2.5 billion but eventually came out at a massive £9 billion. The Government could recover that overrun only through track-access charges, which rose four-fold. This was a vicious circle, because Virgin

Rail then needed a much higher subsidy. Railtrack, as already mentioned, ended up being placed in administration, and the project was taken over by Network Rail. Ewan Brown appears to be slightly sceptical about the rail business and wonders if Railtrack was put into administration to get it out of its obligations to Virgin Rail for its failure to upgrade the West Coast main line to the originally agreed specification and to make other improvements to the infrastructure on time.

Keith had taken on personal responsibility for turning around Coach USA. He was responsible for introducing and implementing a substantial package of cost-saving measures, but market trends were moving faster than he and the US team could match. Matters came to a head at a Board meeting in July 2002, culminating in his resignation after 17 months as Chief Executive.

The old order on the West Coast main line. A pair of Class 87 electric locomotives at London Euston, No 87007 *City of Manchester* leading. *Brian Morrison*

A Bombardier Class 221 'Super Voyager' of Virgin CrossCountry when almost new at Cardiff in April 2003. The ancient timber-fronted canopy over the platform looks incongruous with such a modern train.

By early 2005 the vast majority of electrified services on the West Coast main line were in the hands of Class 390 'Pendolino' tilting trains. The last unit of the order was delivered on 10 March 2005. In the same month the tilting mechanism on the 'Pendolino' fleet won the UK Railway Industry Innovation Award.

People within Stagecoach talk very highly of Keith. Ewan Brown described him as an absolutely excellent finance director but wondered on reflection if it was correct to burden him with the role of Chief Executive. The news of Keith's departure rocked the City, with the shares falling to 30p, but, fortunately, the Group's bankers kept faith.

Brian resumed day-to-day control of Stagecoach, with Robert Speirs becoming non-Executive Chairman. Robert Speirs was a former Group Finance Director of the Royal Bank of Scotland and had been on the Board of Stagecoach since March 1995. He said at the time that the Board had asked for a full review of the Coach USA business.

Martin Griffiths, another former Andersen man, had joined the Stagecoach financial team in 1997 at the age of 31 and soon became Business Development Manager, working closely with Brian and Keith. He was *au fait* with the details of many projects, including the acquisition of Citybus in Hong Kong. The Chinese tend to equate age with experience, and Martin found himself being described as Brian's slave! He also spent nearly three months on the proposed deal with the Vinella family and the Sogin Group in Italy before that fell through. He was nevertheless in the right place at the right time, because he was promoted to Finance Director when Keith moved up to Chief Executive. He laughs about the time, just after his appointment, when Brian introduced him to some analysts, asking them why he should pay £300,000 a year for a Finance Director when he could get a 'wee laddie' to do the job for a fraction of the salary!

When he was Executive Chairman Brian had been advising his people what he thought they ought to do with Coach USA. As already mentioned, he knew that

its operations were spread widely all over the United States and in Canada and that they were involved in a wide variety of work. Back in the driving seat, he soon came to the conclusion that they were not very good at some of it, even though 550 jobs had been cut and a number of cost savings achieved in Keith's time.

Brian drew a line on the map from Chicago to New York. To the south and west of that line 70% of Coach USA's business was leisure-dependent (or 'discretional'), the other 30% being scheduled, contracted or own-brand work, for instance regular commuter services. To the north and east of the line the proportions were reversed. Coach USA could not so easily forecast the revenues from the leisure part of its business and was not recession-proof, and that was the principal reason for the profit warnings.

Brian's strategy, accepted by the Board, was to retain the North East division and to sell all the businesses south and west of the Chicago–New York line. The corporate office in Houston was closed, and the remaining regional managers reported direct to Perth. Roger Bowker had by this time returned from Sweden and moved to the States to implement Brian's strategy.

In October 2002 Stagecoach had to warn the City that the soft US economy and an increasingly competitive market could result in Coach USA's operating profits being substantially lower than those of the previous year. One month later the value of Coach USA was written down by a further £575 million. As a result the Group's shares plunged to an all-time low of 10p, prompting senior executives to talk about 'staring into the abyss'.

There was widespread speculation that Brian might be tempted to buy back the company and take it private, but he always denied that intention. There was also speculation that a rival bidder might try to buy Stagecoach, much of the business being sound and profitable, but that did not happen because of the substantial family holdings, which could block most takeover bids, while for once in his career Brian probably had reason to be grateful for the presence of the OFT and the MMC! As it turned out, this was the lowest point in the history of Stagecoach, and the Group now started to recover.

Brian, Martin, Linda Bell and an in-house team of lawyers set about selling large parts of Coach USA. In May 2003 the Transit business, operating in 35 locations with 1,200 vehicles and 2,000 employees, was sold to a US subsidiary of FirstGroup, for £13.2 million. Taxi operations in three cities were sold in the same month. One month later further parts were sold, including five coach fleets in the northeast states and 255 vehicles to Peter Pan Bus Lines for £24.5 million.

In June 2003 the South Central and West regions of Coach USA were sold to a newly formed affiliate of Kohlberg & Co, a private equity house, for £93.7 million. In the following month the South East region was bought by a joint venture, including the management team, for £29.6 million, and in September the taxi operations in Texas went to a private investment group, for £17.3 million.

Apart from some further small disposals, this left Coach USA with a sound business running commuter, contract and sightseeing services in New York and New Jersey and a contract and commuter business in Chicago. Ewan Brown credits Brian with having done a very good job in down-sizing Coach USA and having found buyers for all the unwanted parts. Martin Griffiths says that, if the action had not been taken, Stagecoach would have bled to death!

Meanwhile Brian's fertile mind came up with yet another imaginative new idea to grow the British bus business. The Government sought advice from the operating industry about how to get best value from its subsidies for the bus industry, which, incidentally, were far below the levels of subsidy in most Continental European countries. Brian focused on routes that were marginal but had potential for organic growth. In the autumn of 2002 he started talking to the Minister of Transport, Alistair Darling, about his proposal to 'Kick Start' routes that were marginal and could be at risk of being abandoned. He proposed that Government funding of £140 million be made available to provide service enhancements over a three-year period; operators would have to submit bids for funding and commit to providing new low-floor vehicles, the aim being to make Kick Start routes commercially viable within that three-year period. Within a year the Department for Transport (and, later, the Scottish Executive) adopted the Kick Start concept and allocated public funding for such projects. Stagecoach successfully introduced new services in areas as diverse as Chesterfield, Devon and Thanet.

In November 2002 the Strategic Rail Authority cut the franchise period for South West Trains from the original 20 years to just three, commencing in February 2004, with an option of an extension for a further two years. On the plus side, SWT retained the Waterloo–Exeter and Reading–Brighton services, which had been due to be transferred to a new Wessex Trains franchise. The SRA explained that the reduction in the duration of the franchise was intended to make the company focus on improving its performance as quickly as possible. Brian welcomed the deal, saying that SWT could prioritise on passenger-service delivery and operational efficiency while the SRA took an equally important role in driving vital infrastructure improvements, such as extending suburban platforms to enable the use of longer trains.

On the subject of train lengths, at peak periods SWT used to run two four-car units coupled together to form eight-car trains, splitting them for off-peak services. However, this was identified as one of the prime causes of delays, so in the spring of 2003 the practice was stopped, even though it resulted in an increase in costs of around £2 million per annum.

Although resolving the problems at Coach USA had been the top priority, Stagecoach was also monitoring developments in other parts of the world. The political situation in Hong Kong was changing, and the Citybus network was coming under increasing pressure from rail construction projects. The Board decided that further growth in Hong Kong would be difficult without considerable capital expenditure, so in June 2003 Citybus was sold to Delta Pearl, a company with close links to New World First Bus, leaving this and the long-established Kowloon Motor Bus as the two remaining major operators in Hong Kong.

Stagecoach received £176 million for Citybus, knowing that Delta Pearl would be able to rationalise the combined operations and that there would be some surplus mid-life double-deck buses available. These were tri-axle Volvo Olympians with Alexander bodywork, built in 1993/4. A deal was struck to bring some of them back to the UK, where they were converted for use on yet another bright idea, the first wholly internet-based express service, Megabus.com.

Coach USA invested in a fleet of 20 new open-top double-deck buses for sightseeing in New York. The first of the batch called at Edinburgh Castle before crossing the Atlantic. It had a Dennis Trident 3 chassis and bodywork by Alexander that included air-conditioning on the lower deck. These buses, meeting the latest emissions legislation, were very welcome in New York, because they replaced elderly vehicles that were nowhere near as environmentally friendly.

Stagecoach brought back around 75 tri-axle Leyland Olympians from Kowloon Motor Bus and Citybus, both in Hong Kong, in 2004 and refurbished them for Megabus.com services. No 13609 (J701 HMY), new in 1990, had been very well maintained. It is seen with a nearly full complement of passengers at Cotteridge, a southern suburb of Birmingham, in April 2004.

Low-cost airlines had established a business model whereby passengers who booked further ahead and who avoided the busiest days — Fridays, Saturdays and Sundays — could secure flights at extremely low prices. Those headline prices attracted a lot of business, but passengers soon learned that the nearer they booked to the date of departure, the higher the fare was likely to be. Even so, the highest fares are usually still very competitive when compared with the full-service airlines. The low-cost airlines also maximised the use of their aircraft, often achieving a turnaround time on the ground of 25-30 minutes — half the time normally taken by the full-service carriers — and pioneered another trend: they encouraged passengers to book on the internet, levying a handling charge on those who wanted to use a booking agent. As more and more people gained access to the internet the percentage of on-line bookings rose dramatically.

Brian believed that there was an opportunity for a low-cost inter-city bus service, initially over medium distances. Sophisticated computer systems were established to handle bookings, control fare structures and monitor takings. Seats could only be secured on-line, and those who booked furthest ahead generally got the lowest fares.

The first service, with six journeys per day, started on 11 August 2003 between Oxford and London. The choice of route was surprising, because it pitched Megabus.com against Stagecoach's highly successful Oxford Tube and a strong competitor in Go-Ahead.

Among the vehicles converted for Megabus.com services were two of the original tri-axle double-deckers bought by Stagecoach in 1989; with a top speed around 48mph they are known by their drivers as 'the slug' and 'the snail'! Further high-capacity tri-axle double-deckers, obtained from Hong Kong, were fitted with high-backed seats and, in some cases, toilets.

Within a year a network of services had been established in Scotland and various parts of England, including a number of routes to London. National Express responded to the competition with some special fare offers, but research by Stagecoach found that many of the passengers would previously have made their journeys by rail or in their own cars.

In June 2003, commenting on its annual results for the year to April, Brian said that Stagecoach was recovering. Its strategy would no longer be to grow by acquisition but to look for opportunities to expand its core businesses in bus and rail in the UK, the United States and New Zealand.

Although Network Rail represented a considerable improvement over Railtrack there was still some friction with SWT. A major effort had been made to improve the reliability of the trains, and this was reflected in higher punctuality figures, but an even better performance was being prevented by problems with the infrastructure. The two companies therefore set up a joint control centre at Waterloo, adopting a team approach to improving still further performance on the SWT network.

Network Rail promised improvements when it started to take maintenance work in-house towards the end of 2003. It was advised by Graham, who had been nominated by the Association of Train Operating Companies to work with Network Rail on their behalf and to secure improvements in communication between the two sides; in particular the Train Operating Companies wanted greater notice of impending track works, so that they could minimise disruption to their services. Graham spends around four days per month in this capacity.

In October 2003 Stagecoach embarked upon a large-scale six-month trial of a fuel additive in 1,000 of its British bus fleet. Cerulean International of Oxford had developed a fuel additive, Envirox, which it claimed would give up to 10% reduction in fuel consumption. The trials produced 5% overall savings, and before the end of 2004 Stagecoach announced that Envirox would be used in all its British buses.

In October 2003 another completely different kind of service, Yellow Taxibus, was started in Scotland, using a number of eight-seat Mercedes-Benz Vito minibuses for demand-responsive transport between Dunfermline, the Ferry Toll Park & Ride centre (just north of the Forth Road Bridge) and Edinburgh. Passengers rang a central control number, as little as half an hour before their desired departure, and were carried from door to door. Fares were higher than on bus services on the same route but were considerably lower than the cost of a taxi. Some of the highest demand came in the evenings, from people who had been out in Edinburgh.

During 2003 Stagecoach introduced yet another initiative to try to increase passenger growth on selected routes in the British market when a direct telephone-based marketing scheme was piloted in Perth and Grimsby, the aim being to contact residents who did not normally use buses. People who showed interest were given the option of a free Megarider ticket, offering them a week's unlimited local travel to sample the services; after a six-week period they were contacted again, to ascertain their opinions. Residents in both towns said that they were impressed, and Stagecoach was able to report a 9% modal shift from car use. No doubt the increasing cost and difficulty of parking in town centres contributed to the growth.

In 2003 the UK came into line with most other countries in the European Union by permitting the use of rigid vehicles longer than the previous limit of 12m. Stagecoach duly borrowed a 13.7m double-decker and tested it on the Oxford–London route, the main reason being to check whether it could get into and out of Oxford's Gloucester Green bus station. An order was then placed with Neoplan for 25 Skyliners, fully air-conditioned, wheelchair-accessible and fitted with 81 reclining seats, for delivery in 2004.

In 2004 Stagecoach completely upgraded the Oxford Tube fleet with 25 Neoplan Skyliners, built to an overall length of 13.7m. The main passenger entrance was just ahead of the second, driven axle, giving access to 63 seats on the upper deck and 18 below. These coaches carry their own distinctive version of the corporate livery; this one is seen at Hyde Park Corner in London in September 2004.

In 2003 Dunfermline depot acquired 13 Mercedes-Benz Vito minibuses, seating eight passengers, for on-demand Taxibus services connecting parts of West Fife with Edinburgh, across the Forth Road Bridge. Fares were higher than those of bus services, because of the convenience of door-to-door travel, but lower than those of taxis. No 60006 (SW03 OYG) was photographed in the Scottish capital in July 2004.

East London kept its Routemasters in very good condition, right to the end of operation. By now numbered 12723 in the corporate scheme, the former RML2723 (SMK 723F) was photographed running into Trafalgar Square in August 2003, looking well for its 35 years.

More Megabus.com services were opened in Scotland, linking Edinburgh, Glasgow, Dundee and St Andrews. They proved particularly popular with 'silver surfers'; Perth Library, tongue in cheek, telephoned the Stagecoach headquarters to say that its computers were being hogged by grandmothers booking Megabus.com travel!

There was further activity with British rail franchises in the spring of 2004. Stagecoach had decided which franchises were of interest and which were not, Graham stating that it was not interested in PTE railways because they did not give the Group the opportunity to use its flair; it preferred commuter and express services. The Strategic Rail Authority had taken back the South East franchise from Connex and was running it while looking for a new franchise-holder. Stagecoach applied but did not make the shortlist; it then teamed up with DSB (Danish State Railways), which had, and they agreed to make a joint bid, DSB obviously benefiting from the Stagecoach knowledge of the UK market.

Soon afterwards Stagecoach and Virgin Rail teamed up with Deutsche Bahn, the German state rail company, in a second attempt to take over the East Coast franchise from GNER. Collectively, they thought that they could deliver a stronger and more powerful bid. The German rail giant recognised that there was an increasing global trend towards deregulating railways and joined the consortium to gain vital experience. However, in August DB pulled out, concerned about the cost of covering its contingent liabilities. Virgin Rail and Stagecoach continued with their bid,

as equal partners in Inter City Railways (*i.e.* not as Virgin Rail). The successful bidder will be expected to continue with existing trains that are already quite elderly. Graham believes that the next franchise that will call for new trains will be Great Western. He predicts that there will be a steady reduction in the number of franchises, through amalgamation, as has already occurred; in his view there should be no more than 12-14 rail operators.

In July 2004 the Government announced plans to improve the structure of the rail industry and ensure that it works in the collective best interests of passengers, taxpayers and investors. Many of the ideas outlined three years previously in Stagecoach's policy paper, 'A Platform for Change', had gathered a lot of support and were incorporated in the Government's policy.

The integration of infrastructure maintenance into Network Rail was practically complete, and the joint control centre at Waterloo — the first in the country — was working well. The Group said that further vertical integration was essential if the Government was to optimise both the cost and performance of the UK rail industry, while informal arrangements between Network Rail and the Train Operating Companies should be formalised.

Back on the buses, the telemarketing initiative was used next on selected routes at Stagecoach Manchester. The fleet had reported a 2.2% increase in overall patronage across its network during 2003 but was looking for growth of around 10% on some specifically targeted routes. In another initiative the

The Designline Olymbus hybrid bus, built in New Zealand on a MAN low-entry chassis, was brought across principally to demonstrate to Tyne & Wear PTE, but Stagecoach showed it to several local authorities in other parts of the country. The bus is seen in September 2004, outside the offices of Warwickshire County Council. A Capstone micro-turbine engine, mounted at the rear, provides power to a generator that in turn feeds current to banks of batteries which drive the rear wheels through an electric motor.

Manchester subsidiary introduced a revised timetable during the school and university summer holidays, because shorter journey times were possible between the suburbs and the city centre; it also avoided the risk of drivers' running early in lighter traffic.

In another interesting development Stagecoach brought over from New Zealand a hybrid diesel-electric bus, initially to demonstrate to Tyne & Wear PTE, which was interested in using vehicles of this type on its Quayside Transit project. The vehicle was built by Designline on a 14-gross-tonne low-floor MAN chassis. An LPG-fuelled Capstone turbine provided power to a generator that in turn passed electric current to a series of batteries. The rear axle was driven by an electric traction motor. Whenever the vehicle braked energy was regenerated to the batteries, helping to keep them charged. It was found that the hybrid bus could run largely in all-electric mode and that it was very quiet. Stagecoach subsequently won a tender to operate the route, for which another nine buses were due to be delivered in 2005.

In 2004 Warwickshire County Council bought four TransBus Enviro 300 low-floor buses and contracted the operation of a regular service between Rugby and Leamington Spa to Stagecoach. The last of the quartet is seen in Leamington in September of that year.

Towards the end of 2003 six TransBus Trident low-floor double-deckers with the Plaxton President style of bodywork, built in the former Northern Counties factory in Wigan, were delivered to Oxford and painted in a dedicated livery for services to and from Oxford Brookes University. No 18052 (KX53 VNC) was one of three Stagecoach buses in this scene in Oxford in May 2004. Although, at first glance, it looks similar to the Alexander ALX400 body, the Plaxton model had rectangular headlights, while those on the Alexander were circular.

Thirty of the 2003 TransBus Tridents with Wigan-built bodywork were delivered to Stagecoach Manchester. By March 2004, when 18048 (MX53 FMU) was photographed in Manchester, the Group-wide fleet-numbering system was becoming widely used and can be seen here prominently below the windscreen.

In June 2004 Stagecoach reported excellent financial results for the year to 30 April. Operating profits were up to £148 million, while net debt had tumbled from £780 million at the height of the Coach USA crisis to just £67.6 million. Shareholders, including Brian and Ann, who had taken a battering in the previous four years, were rewarded with the return of £250 million of capital. The share price recovered. Brian said that Stagecoach was entering an exciting new phase. The renewed focus, combined with strong cash-generative qualities and a substantially 'de-risked' portfolio, meant there was real potential to drive the Group forward.

Turnover in the two London fleets was up by 19.1%, partly reflecting the addition of new routes when Congestion Charging was introduced in the centre of the capital; the use of cars fell by nearly 20% and many people transferred to bus services. Although Stagecoach is happy with its London business it prefers the deregulated model, because that gives the Group freedom to develop its own new initiatives and grow revenues even more.

The only dark cloud on the horizon was the Virgin Rail Cross Country franchise. It had been operating on a 'cost-plus' contract with the Strategic Rail Authority and was one of the most heavily subsidised franchises in the country. Although Virgin Rail thought it was close to securing a new franchise through to 2012 the SRA ended those talks in August, saying that the offer did not represent value for money. There was speculation that Cross Country would be broken up and down-sized, abandoning the longer routes and requiring passengers to change trains at various major junctions. At the time of writing Virgin Rail is still waiting to hear how the SRA intends to proceed.

In October 2004 Stagecoach reported that the Megabus.com network had carried more than 1 million passengers in its first 14 months and that use of the network had grown by 400% since March. The trend was towards longer-distance corridors such as Newcastle/Leeds, Liverpool and Cheltenham/Gloucester to London; some of the shorter routes had been closed down.

Although fitted with toilets the former Hong Kong double-deckers were not ideal for Megabus work, so Stagecoach placed an order with Neoplan for a further 25 13.7m 91-seat double-deck coaches, delivered from January 2005. These are bound to increase greatly the appeal of the Megabus.com services, with further routes likely to be added in the summer of 2005.

In December Stagecoach announced strong results for the half-year, whereupon the share price rose quite sharply, to 114p.

In the same month Stagecoach revealed that it was in discussions with Siemens over its optical-guidance system for buses (developed originally for the advanced CIVIS vehicle of Irisbus), whereby a camera, mounted above the windscreen, follows two intermittent parallel lines painted on the road surface. The system controls the steering with great accuracy, enabling a bus to park only 40mm from a kerb at the same height as the floor of the bus. The driver can override the system in an emergency. Stagecoach believes that the system can be used on conventional buses in heritage cities where traffic is very congested.

Just before the end of the year the OFT cleared the joint Stagecoach/Virgin Rail bid for the East Coast main line, subject to certain undertakings. The partners had argued that rail services carried only 6% of traffic between London and Scotland — far lower than the numbers carried by the airlines. A rival bid by FirstGroup was also referred to the OFT.

On 12 December 2004 South West Trains implemented a major new timetable across its network. Traffic patterns had been examined very closely, taking

In 2003/4 Stagecoach bought 100 TransBus Darts with Pointer 2 bodywork for service in fleets outside London. This one joined Midland Red South and was branded for the Atherstone–Coventry route. It is seen in the latter city in April 2004. Note the closeness in height between the kerb and the floor of the bus, making it very easy for passengers with reduced mobility and mothers with buggies to get on and off.

Above: By February 2004 M680 TDB, numerically the first of the 20 Dennis Dragon double-deckers that returned from Kenya in 1999, had started its third life. It was fitted with more comfortable high-back seats and entered service on the relatively short-lived Manchester–Leeds route of Megabus.com. Although the vinyls appear to obscure vision for passengers inside the vehicle, in fact, they can see out quite easily. This bus is seen in Leeds in February 2004.

Right: The Megabus service proved so successful that it was decided to commence upgrading with an order for 25 Neoplan Skyliners similar to those already delivered for the Oxford Tube. No 50126 (SV54 ELC) is seen heading for London in March 2005.

into account changing demographics. Some stations were given more frequent services, while those to others were cut back. Wherever possible, all routes were converted to clock-face timetables, which are always popular with passengers.

Graham feels that a lot of hard work has achieved results at SWT and that it is probably now regarded as the class act among London commuter-rail franchises. The culture of many rail managers had to change; they always loved running trains but have now learned to satisfy customers as well. SWT has more secure stations than any other network, and security on trains themselves has also been greatly improved; the new 'Desiro' trains are fitted with closed-circuit television, enabling the guard to view all carriages. Every station on the network has real-time information, activated automatically from the signalling system.

One of the challenges in writing this book has been bringing it to a conclusion. With Stagecoach being one of the world's leading private-sector transport operators, my publisher and I face the challenge that there will be further developments before the book is published; if that happens, we can only ask for your understanding.

The next, brief chapter looks at the Stagecoach philosophy, how it is run today and where it might be heading.

Above: Transport for London started to specify articulated buses for some high-capacity routes running through Central London. Mercedes-Benz had sufficient capacity in its vast Mannheim factory to be able to deliver buses within the lead times required by TfL for the start of new services. Stagecoach took its first batch of 35 Citaro articulated buses in 2003, and this one is seen in Trafalgar Square in April 2004. They had only 49 seats but a high capacity for standing passengers travelling short distances. Passengers had to buy their tickets before boarding the bus or use multi-journey passes.

Left: The welcome upgrading of South West Trains' London commuter services commenced in 2004 with the delivery of Class 444 and Class 450 'Desiro' trains. One of the latter, No 450082, is seen when freshly into service, showing its blue livery and dual-width plug doors. *Brian Morrison*

Above: A Stagecoach standard Volvo B10M with Alexander PS bodywork waits for its next turn of duty at Whiting Bay, on Arran, in June 2003. Although the current requirement, quite rightly, is for buses with a large part of the floor only one step above the ground, this view clearly shows the three shallow steps onto the main floor of the B10M/Alexander. These buses have proved to be very reliable workhorses.

Top right: Looking very smart in the current corporate colours in Cardiff in December 2004, No 52277 (M917WJK) was a Volvo B10M-62 with Plaxton Expressliner bodywork, dating from 1995. Regular express services have proved very popular with passengers in several parts of the country.

Lower right: Stagecoach placed large orders with TransBus for Dennis Darts with Plaxton Pointer 2 bodywork, delivered in 2004. No 34668 (CN54 EDO) was branded for regular services between Caerphilly and Cardiff and is seen in the Welsh capital in December 2004.

This Dennis Dart with Plaxton Pointer bodywork had a tragically short life with Stagecoach. Seen in its home town of Carlisle, it was written off in the disastrous floods which swamped the Stagecoach depot in the city in January 2005, when the River Eden burst its banks. In the small hours of the morning the river surged through an adjacent sewage works and smashed parked buses against each other and into the depot, filling them with badly contaminated water more than halfway up the main window line. All the buses that were in the depot had to be written off.

Stagecoach is supporting the bid for London to host the Olympic Games in 2012. The proposals include building a number of venues in the territory of the East London subsidiary. No 18208 (LX04 FWU) is seen in Oxford Street in October 2004.

A further batch of Mercedes-Benz Citaro articulated buses, operated from a purpose-built depot at Waterden Road, Stratford, was placed into service in June 2004 on East London's busy route 25 between Oxford Circus and Ilford. No 23041 (LX04 KZN) is seen approaching Tottenham Court Road station as night falls.

Stagecoach Today

EW companies have achieved as much in 25 years as Stagecoach. In its early years, as an upstart in the industry, it was loved by its customers and loathed by its nationalised competitors, who are no more; indeed, some parts are now in the Stagecoach empire.

Stagecoach then went through a turbulent period, growing rapidly and taking full advantage of the privatisation of public-sector bus companies, mainly in the UK, but also elsewhere. There were regular clashes with the authorities, which, frequently, did not deal Stagecoach an even hand.

Flotation enabled Stagecoach to grow dramatically, with the City encouraging the Group to go into all kinds of transport ventures. From that time it evolved from being a large family business into a quoted corporation. The combined business skills of Brian and (until her retirement) Ann, allied with the specialist skills of their managers, created a very dynamic company. Brian continued to lead and develop this team until taking a back seat as Executive Chairman, removing himself from day-to-day management responsibilities. At that point Stagecoach became more like any other large corporation.

Looking back, Brian admits that the period from 2000 to 2002 was the accident-prone stage, when Stagecoach went on a roller-coaster and the share price plunged. Although the City fell out of love with Stagecoach in a very big way Brian says that he does not have any issues with the Square Mile. During this phase the corporate structure began to constrict the entrepreneurial flair for which Stagecoach was and still is so famous.

The years 2003 and 2004 saw a restoration of the Group's culture and credibility and the revitalisation of its strategic planning. The remaining parts of the North American business are running well, the UK bus business continues to experience growth, even outside London, thanks to the regular introduction of new and innovative ideas, and there has been some re-positioning in rail franchising, with more likely to follow.

There is a refreshing informality about Stagecoach. It is unencumbered by the large central functions and empire-builders that constitute an overhead in many large organisations. Of course, informality should not be confused with any lack of functionality or responsibility. Stagecoach thrives on delegation and short chains of command, and any supplier will confirm that Stagecoach is a hard negotiator.

Some ill-informed people still go on about Stagecoach being ruthless. That might have been justifiable some years ago, in a very limited number of cases, but it is certainly no longer the case today, and the Group

The 'Voyager' units can be seen the length and breadth of Britain, from Aberdeen to Brighton and even Penzance, on cross-country services which avoid the need to change trains in London. Class 221 'Super Voyager' No 221123 is seen passing through Southampton on 24 May 2004. *Brian Morrison*

has among the best relations in the industry with its employees and trade unions.

Stagecoach does not enter the territory of another operator unless its sees an opportunity to introduce a new kind of service, potentially winning new customers. Two recent examples that come to mind are the direct services between Glasgow city centre and selected suburbs, using the motorway network, and Megabus.com. On the other hand, if a competitor comes into Stagecoach territory it can expect a fight. Usually a competitor will abstract enough traffic to make the service of the incumbent operator unprofitable, and it is perfectly within the law for Stagecoach — or any other resident operator — to defend its territory by competing vigorously with any invader.

Stagecoach's days as a highly acquisitive company are probably over, but that does not rule out any acquisitions which make a particularly good fit with the present business. Various bus subsidiaries in the UK have taken over small operators in their territory, but even with the smallest transactions there is always the risk of an investigation by the competition authorities; Stagecoach has found that even the acquisition of a fleet of less than 10 vehicles has attracted their attention.

Any larger-scale consolidation of the British bus industry is unlikely, partly because Transport for London does not want any contractor to have more than 25% of the market in the capital and partly because the competition authorities would be unwilling to see any of the large groups become more dominant than they already are in the major conurbations.

Ewan Brown, the longest-serving non-executive director, talks about the Board management of Stagecoach, saying that the quality of papers is considerably better than that of those he receives from other companies. The Board meets about seven times a year, and meetings usually last no longer than four hours. The balance of discussion between reporting and strategic matters is, in his view, as it should be. All issues are discussed in a very open manner, and a lot of time is spent looking forward.

He praises Bob Speirs, saying that he has had long experience at main-Board level and that Stagecoach is fortunate to have him as Chairman. It is a sign of the times that Health & Safety, part of Graham's remit, has been the first item on the Board agenda for the last two years or so.

Martin Griffiths talks about how Stagecoach is run today. It is still very lean, with short lines of communication. As Finance Director Martin runs a series of checks and balances on performance, helped by strong divisional managers. All reporting is on four-week cycles. Each subsidiary has to prepare a complete financial justification for every new bus that it wants. At the end of the chain, any bus that is withdrawn is normally first offered around other subsidiaries before being sold off.

There is a typical Scottish canniness with money. People are careful how they spend it at Stagecoach. Although there is a lot of delegated responsibility, one senses that people treat the money as if it were their own. This is understandable, because quite a number are shareholders, but it is, nevertheless, highly commendable.

The final word must be about Brian. Several of his senior directors have said, in a very good-humoured way, that they never knew what bright idea was going to be bounced off them on a Monday morning, after Brian had returned from his weekend break. Martin said that the trick was to distil the good ideas from the indifferent and the impractical. Many of them have got through those barriers. Brian encourages analysis of his ideas and those of others, saying that Stagecoach has distinguished itself by so frequently being the first in the industry to develop new initiatives. Think about Megarider, Kick Start, Envirox, telemarketing, Citi, Yellow Taxibus, electric buses, Megabus.com, optically guided buses, to name but a few.

We can expect to see many more bright ideas that pass the internal tests and help to grow the businesses in the Group portfolio. The senior management is comparatively young; Brian has only recently turned 50. They work as a team and have the skill and energy to take Stagecoach forward into its next 25 years.

Clock-face timetables, brand-new vehicles and easy-to-understand route branding have all combined to increase passenger numbers. Even the smallest buses on the market today, like this Midland Red South Optare Solo M850, are now wheelchair-accessible and have become very popular with passengers, because most of the floor is only one step above the ground.

Left: Stagecoach has encouraged the preservation in running order of a number of interesting vehicles from its early days. Nowadays a member of the special-event fleet, Volvo B58/Duple FES 831W was the very first vehicle bought new by Stagecoach, in 1981.

Left: Although Alexander (Northern) never operated any Bristol single-deckers, MW6G/ECW HDV 639E has been preserved by Stagecoach in Bluebird colours, complete with the Bluebird logo and the Royal Warrant.

Below: Looking very smart in the sunshine is HGM 335E, a 1967 Bristol FLF6G with Eastern Coach Works body, originally new to Central SMT and owned by Stagecoach since the early 1980s. These buses were built to an overall length slightly greater than 30ft and therefore seated 44 on the upper deck and 34 downstairs, giving them the same capacity as the first generation of rear-engined double-deckers.